Stories of Favorite Hymns

Stories
of
Favorite
Hymns

Kenneth W. Osbeck

FAMILY
CHRISTIAN
PRESS

Stories of Favorite Hymns

© 2002 by Kenneth W. Osbeck

Published by Family Christian Press, Grand Rapids, MI by special arrangement with Kregel Publications, P.O. Box 2607, Grand Rapids, Michigan 49501.

ISBN 1-930871-49-X

Printed in the United States of America

1 2 3 4 5 6 / 06 05 04 03 02

Contents

All Creatures of Our God and King

*All Thy works shall praise Thee, O Lord; and Thy
saints shall bless Thee. They shall speak of the glory
of Thy kingdom, and talk of Thy power.*

—Psalm 145:10–11

Author—Francis of Assisi, 1182–1226
English Translation—William H. Draper, 1855–1933
Music—From the *Geistliche Kirchengesäng* of 1623
Tune Name—"Lasst Uns Erfreuen"
Meter—LMA (88.88 with Alleluias)
Scripture Reference—Psalm 145

All Creatures of Our God and King

This inspiring expression of praise found in nearly every hymnal was originally written in 1225 by one of the most interesting figures in all of church history. Giovanni Bernardone, who was better known as Saint Francis of Assisi, was a mystic, medieval monk who spent his lifetime as an itinerant evangelist, preaching and helping the poor people of Italy.

Saint Francis was born in Assisi, Italy, in 1182. After an early self-indulgent life as a soldier, he reformed his ways dramatically, at the age of twenty-five, and determined to serve God by imitating the selfless life of Christ in all that he did. Although his family were people of considerable means, Francis scorned the possession of material goods, denounced his inherited wealth, denied himself everything but the most meager necessities, and devoted himself completely to moving about his area as Christ's representative. At the age of twenty-eight Francis founded the influential Franciscan Order of Friars, which developed into a large movement of young men and some women who adopted his religious beliefs and ascetic style of life.

Saint Francis was known as a great lover of nature, seeing the hand of God in all creation. One of the well-known master paintings from this time was done by the famous Italian artist. Giotto, and shows Saint Francis feeding the birds. The following well-known verse was written in tribute to this man:

> Saint Francis came to preach—with smiles he met the
> friendless, fed the poor, freed a trapped bird, led home
> a child; Although he spoke no word—his text, God's
> love, the town did not forget.

There are many interesting but strange incidents and legends associated with the life of Saint Francis which are difficult to explain. Historical accounts relate various visitations that Saint Francis is supposed to have had with the Lord. One of those occasions was while Francis was fasting for forty days in the lofty mountain of LaVerne. It is said that this encounter left him for the remainder of his life bearing on his hands, feet, and body the stigmata or painful wounds of the crucified Lord. Another account, whether fact or fiction, states that as his soul was being committed to the creator, a flock of larks gathered unmistakably about his little hut and rose, singing a beautiful song in the still evening air.

"All Creatures of Our God and King" is from another of Saint Francis's writings entitled "Canticles of the Sun," said to have been written one hot summer day in 1225, one year before his death, while Francis was very ill and suffering the loss of his eyesight. Throughout his life Saint Francis made much use of singing and believed strongly in the importance of church music. In all he wrote more than sixty hymns for use in the monastery. This beautiful expression of praise is one that has survived the passing of these several hundred years.

The English translation of this text was made by William Draper, a village rector in England, who prepared this paraphrased version for a children's choir festival at some time between 1899–1919. The tune for this text first appeared in a Roman Catholic hymnal in Cologne, Germany, in 1623. After being forgotten for a time, the tune was revived in the present century and appeared in the *English Hymnal,* published in London, England, in 1906. An interesting congregational use of this hymn is to sing it as a two, three, or four part round or canon. This can be done simply by disregarding the hold or fermata at the end of the second line. Another interesting practice is to sing the alternating phrases antiphonally.

Although there is much that is difficult to understand and explain about the author of this text, we certainly can be thankful that God ordained the birth, translation, and the preservation of this fine expression of praise for His people to enjoy even to the present time.

It should be noted that the Keswick Doxology, "Praise God from Whom All Blessings Flow," with the alleluias, can be used effectively with this tune.

2

Amazing Grace

*For by grace are ye saved through faith; and that
not of yourselves; it is the gift of God: not of works,
lest any man should boast.*

—Ephesians 2:8–9

Author—John Newton, 1725–1807
Music—From Carrell and Clayton's "Virginia Harmony," 1831
Tune Name—"Amazing Grace"
Meter—CM (86.86)
Scripture Reference—1 Chronicles 17:16–17

Amazing Grace

1. A - maz - ing grace! how sweet the sound That saved a wretch like me! I once was lost, but now am found; Was blind, but now I see.

2. 'Twas grace that taught my heart to fear, And grace my fears re - lieved. How pre - cious did that grace ap - pear The hour I first be - lieved!

3. The Lord has prom - ised good to me; His word my hope se - cures. He will my shield and por - tion be As long as life en - dures.

4. Thro' man - y dan - gers, toils, and snares I have al - read - y come. 'Tis grace hath bro't me safe thus far, And grace will lead me home.

5. When we've been there ten thou - sand years, Bright, shin - ing as the sun, We've no less days to sing God's praise Than when we'd first be - gun.

In a small cemetery of a parish churchyard in Olney, England, stands a granite tombstone with the following inscription: "John Newton, clerk, once an infidel and Libertine, a servant of slavers in Africa, was, by the rich mercy of our Lord and Savior Jesus Christ, preserved, restored, pardoned, and appointed to preach the Faith he had long labored to destroy." This fitting testimonial, written by Newton himself prior to his death, describes aptly the unusual and colorful life of this man, one of the great evangelical preachers of the eighteenth century.

John Newton's mother, a Godly woman, died when he was not quite seven years of age. When his father remarried and after several brief years of formal education away from home; John left school and joined his father's ship, at the age of eleven, to begin life as a seaman. His early years were one continuous round of rebellion and debauchery. After serving on several ships as well as working for a period of time on the islands and mainland of the West African coast collecting slaves for sale to visiting traders, Newton eventually became a captain of his own slave ship. Needless to say, the capturing, selling, and transporting of black slaves to the plantations in the West Indies and America was a cruel and vicious way of life.

On March 10, 1748, while returning to England from Africa during a particularly stormy voyage when it appeared that all would be lost, Newton began reading Thomas à Kempis's book, *Imitation of Christ*. Kempis was a Dutch monk, 1380–1471, who belonged to an order called the Brethren of the Common Life. This book is still printed today as a religious classic. The message of the book and the frightening experience at sea were used by the Holy Spirit to sow the seeds of Newton's eventual conversion and personal acceptance of Christ as his Savior.

For the next several years he continued as a slave ship captain, trying to justify his work by seeking to improve conditions as much as possible, even holding public worship services for his hardened crew of thirty each Sunday. Eventually, however, he felt convicted of the inhuman aspects of this work and became a strong and effective crusader against slavery. Newton returned to England, established a home with his youthful sweetheart, Mary Catlett, whom he had married on February 12, 1750, and became a clerk at the Port of Liverpool for the next nine years. During this period he felt the call of God increasingly to preach the gospel and began to study diligently for the ministry. He was greatly aided and influenced by the evangelist George Whitefield as well as the Wesleys, but he decided to stay within the established Anglican Church rather than to join forces with these Dissenters. At the age of thirty-nine, John Newton was ordained by the Anglican Church and began his first pastorate at the little village of Olney, near Cambridge, England. His work for the next fifteen years (1764–1779) was a most fruitful and influential ministry.

Especially effective was the use of the story of his early life and conversion experience, which he told often. In addition to preaching for the stated services in his own church, Newton would hold services regularly in any large building he could secure in the surrounding area. This was an unheard of practice for an Anglican clergyman of that day. Wherever he preached, large crowds gathered to hear the "Old Converted Sea Captain."

Another of Newton's extremist practices at the Olney Church was the singing of hymns that expressed the simple, heartfelt faith of his preaching rather than the staid singing of the Psalms from the *Sternhold and Hopkins Psalter,* which was practiced in other Anglican churches. When Newton couldn't find enough available hymns for this purpose, he began writing his own. To assist him in this endeavor, he enlisted the aid of his friend and neighbor, William Cowper, a well-known writer of classic literature of this period. In 1779 their combined efforts produced the famous *Olney Hymns* hymnal, one of the most important single contributions made to the field of evangelical hymnody. In this ambitious collection of 349 hymns, sixty-seven were written by Cowper with the remainder by Newton. The purpose of the hymnal, according to Newton's Preface, was "a desire to promote the faith and comfort of sincere Christians."

Since 1947, an interesting ancient tradition has been revived at the Olney Church. It is the annual pancake race that is held on the Tuesday (Shrove Tuesday) prior to the beginning of Lent. The ladies of the parish race from the center of town to the church flipping pancakes. At the service the winner is announced followed by the congregation singing "Amazing Grace" and other Olney Hymnal favorites.

After concluding his ministry at Olney, Newton spent the remaining twenty-eight years of his life as pastor of the influential St. Mary Woolnoth Church in London. Among his converts there was Claudius Buchanan, who became a missionary to the East Indies, and Thomas Scott, the Bible commentator. By this time Newton had also established a strong relationship with William Wilberforce and other political leaders engaged in the crusade for the abolition of the slave trade. It is interesting to note that the year of Newton's death, 1807, was the same year that the British Parliament finally abolished slavery throughout all of its domain.

In 1790 Newton's wife, beloved companion for forty years, died of cancer. Mary had been a wife of true devotion and encouragement, but now John faced the next seventeen long years without her. In 1893 John and Mary's remains were reinterred in the Olney Church graveyard, where the massive granite monument can still be viewed.

Until the time of his death at the age of eighty-two, John Newton never ceased to marvel at God's mercy and grace that had so dramatically changed his life. This was the dominant theme of his preaching and writing. Shortly before his death a spokesman for the church suggested that he consider retirement because of failing health, eyesight, and memory. Newton replied, "What, shall the old Africa blasphemer stop while he can still speak?" On another occasion before his death he is quoted as proclaiming with a loud voice during a message, "My memory is nearly gone, but I remember two things: That I am a great sinner and that Christ is a great Savior!"

Undoubtedly, the most representative expression of John Newton's life is his appealing hymn, "Amazing Grace." The hymn, originally consisting of six stanzas and entitled "Faith's Review and Expectation," was based on 1 Chronicles 17:16–17. Three interesting additional verses written by Newton that are not included in most hymnals are as follows:

1. The Lord has promised good to me, His Word my hope secures;
   He will my shield and portion be as long as life endures.
2. Yes, when this heart and flesh shall fail, and mortal life shall cease,
   I shall possess within the veil, a life of joy and peace.
3. The earth shall soon dissolve like snow, the sun forbear to shine;
   But God, who called me here below, will be forever mine.

The tune, "Amazing Grace," is an early American folk melody. It was first known as a plantation melody entitled "Loving Lambs." The earliest known publication of this tune was found in a book entitled *The Virginia Harmony,* compiled by James P. Carrell and David S. Clayton and published in 1831 in Winchester, Virginia. Scarcely a hymnal appeared throughout the South during the remainder of the nineteenth century that did not include this hymn.

John Newton also wrote the text for "Glorious Things of Thee Are Spoken."

3

Be Thou My Vision

Where there is no vision, the people perish: but he that keepeth the law, happy is he.

—Proverbs 29:18

Text—Irish hymn, c. 8th century
Translated by Mary E. Byrne, 1880–1931
Versified by Eleanor H. Hull, 1860–1935
Music—Irish Melody
Tune Name—"Slane"
Meter—10 10. 10 10

Be Thou My Vision

1. Be thou my vi - sion, O Lord of my heart;
2. Be thou my wis - dom, and thou my true word;
3. Rich - es I heed not, nor earth's emp - ty praise,
4. High King of heav - en, my vic - to - ry won,

1. nought be all else to me, save that thou art —
2. I ev - er with thee and thou with me, Lord;
3. thou mine in - her - i - tance, now and al - ways:
4. may I reach heav - en's joys, O bright heaven's Sun!

1. thou my best thought, by day or by night,
2. thou my great Fa - ther, thy child let me be;
3. thou and thou on - ly, first in my heart,
4. heart of my own heart, what - ev - er be - fall,

1. wak - ing or sleep - ing, thy pres - ence my light.
2. thou in me dwell - ing, and I one with thee.
3. high King of heav - en, my trea - sure thou art.
4. still be my vi - sion, O rul - er of all.

"Vision is the art of seeing things invisible."
　　　　—Jonathan Swift, *Thoughts on Various Subjects*

"Give us clear vision that we may know where to stand
and what to stand for, because unless we stand for something, we shall fall for anything."
　　　　—Peter Marshall, *Mr. Jones, Meet the Master*

This eighth-century, anonymous, Irish hymn text expresses,
in the quaint Celtic style, the ageless need of man to have a
heavenly vision and to experience God's care and personal pres-
ence throughout this earthly pilgrimage. The author's high
regard for God is evident in the various titles ascribed Him:
Vision, Lord, Best Thought, Wisdom, Word, Great Father, High
King, Inheritance, Treasure, Sun, Ruler, and Heart.

Another interesting verse often omitted in our hymnals is as
follows:

Be Thou my breast-plate, my sword for the fight,
Be Thou my armour, and be Thou my might;
Thou my soul's shelter, and Thou my high tower,
Raise Thou me heavenward, O Power of my Power.

Mary Byrne's translation of this ancient Irish poem into
English prose first appeared in the journal *Erin*, Volume Two,
published in 1905. Later the prose was put into verse form by
Eleanor H. Hull and published in her *Poem Book of the Gael*,
1912. The tune, "Slane," is a traditional Irish air from Patrick
W. Joyce's collection, *Old Irish Folk Music and Songs*, published
in 1909. The tune was originally used with a secular text, "With
My Love on the Road." Its first association with this hymn text
was in the *Irish Church Hymnal* of 1919. The tune is named for
a hill, ten miles from Tara, in County Meath, where St. Patrick
is said to have challenged King Loegaire and the Druid priests

by lighting the Paschal fire on Easter eve. Although the melody has been harmonized by various musicians, it is generally recommended that this tune is most effective when sung in unison.

Mary Elizabeth Byrne was born in Dublin, Ireland, in 1880. She received her education at the University of Dublin and became a research worker and writer for the Board of Intermediate Education in her home town. One of her most important works was her contribution to the *Old and Mid-Irish Dictionary* and the *Dictionary of the Irish Language.*

Eleanor H. Hull was born in Manchester, England, on January 15, 1860. She was the founder and secretary of the Irish Text Society and served as president of the Irish Literary Society, in London. She authored several books on Irish history and literature.

Our visionary attitude throughout life is often the difference between success and mediocrity. One is reminded of the classic story of the two shoe-salesmen who were sent to a primitive island to determine business potential. The first salesman wired back, "Coming home immediately. No one here wears shoes." The second man responded, "Send a boatload of shoes immediately. The possibilities for selling shoes here are unlimited."

May we as believers be characterized as people of vision— "looking unto Jesus, the author and finisher of our faith" (Heb. 12:2a).

4

Blessed Redeemer

And He bearing His cross went forth into a place of a skull, which is called in the Hebrew, Golgotha; Where they crucified Him, and two others with Him, on either side one, and Jesus in the midst.

—John 19:17–18

Author—Avis B. Christiansen, 1895–1985
Composer—Harry Dixon Loes, 1892–1965

Blessed Redeemer

1. Up Cal-v'ry's moun-tain, one dread-ful morn, Walked Christ my Sav-ior,
2. "Fa-ther, for-give them!" thus did He pray, E'en while His life-blood
3. O how I love Him, Sav-ior and Friend! How can my prais-es

wea-ry and worn; Fac-ing for sin-ners death on the cross,
flowed fast a-way; Pray-ing for sin-ners while in such woe—
ev-er find end! Thru years un-num-bered on heav-en's shore,

CHORUS

That He might save them from end-less loss.
No one but Je-sus ev-er loved so. Bless-ed Re-deem-er, pre-cious Re-
My tongue shall praise Him for-ev-er-more.

deem-er! Seems now I see Him on Cal-va-ry's tree, Wound-ed and

bleed-ing, for sin-ners plead-ing—Blind and un-heed-ing— dy-ing for me!

$\mathcal{M}$rs. Avis Christiansen is to be ranked as one of the important gospel hymn writers of the twentieth century. She has written hundreds of gospel hymn texts as well as several volumes of published poems. Mrs. Christiansen states that all of her works have come out of her own Christian experience and express her heart's spiritual desires and convictions. She cannot recall any unusual experiences associated with the writing of these texts, but rather just her daily walk and intimate fellowship with the Lord. Several of her popular favorites include: "Only One Life," "In the Shadow of the Cross," "Only Jesus," "Precious Hiding Place," "Believe on the Lord Jesus Christ," "Love Found a Way," "Only Glory By and By," and many more. She has collaborated with such well-known gospel musicians as Harry Dixon Loes, Homer Hammontree, Lance Latham, George Schuler, Wendell Loveless, Harry Clarke, and Haldor Lillenas.

Mrs. Christiansen was born in Chicago, Illinois, in 1895, and was raised in a Christian home. She was converted to Christ in early childhood. After high school, she attended a secretarial school and later the Moody Bible Institute evening school. She was married to E. O. Christiansen, who was affiliated with the Moody Bible Institute for nearly forty years before his homegoing. Together they raised two daughters. Mrs. Christiansen was a faithful member of the Moody Memorial Church of Chicago since 1915, serving in many varied capacities in the ministry there.

Harry Dixon Loes was born in Kalamazoo, Michigan, on October 20, 1892. After serving several churches as music director and later being active for more than twelve years in evangelistic work, he joined the music faculty of the Moody Bible Institute, in 1939, where he remained as a popular music teacher until his death, in 1965. Mr. Loes was the writer of numerous gospel songs and choruses.

One day while listening to a sermon on the subject of Christ's atonement entitled "Blessed Redeemer," Mr. Loes was inspired to compose this tune. He then sent the melody with the suggested title to Mrs. Christiansen, a friend for many years, asking her to write the text. The hymn first appeared in *Songs of Redemption*, compiled by Mann and Jelks, in 1920, and published by the Baptist Home Mission Board, Atlanta, Georgia.

5

Fairest Lord Jesus

For by Him were all things created, that are in
heaven, and that are in earth, visible and invisible,
whether they be thrones, or dominions, or principali-
ties, or powers: All things were created by Him, and
for Him.

—Colossians 1:16

Text—From *Münster Gesangbuch,* 1677. 4th verse translated by
Joseph A. Seiss, 1823–1904
Music—From *Schlesische Volkslieder,* 1842. Adapted by Richard S.
Willis, 1819–1900
Tune Name—"Crusaders' Hymn"
Meter—568.558

Fairest Lord Jesus

1. Fair - est Lord Je - sus! Rul - er of all na - ture!
2. Fair are the mead - ows, Fair - er still the wood - lands,
3. Fair is the sun - shine, Fair - er still the moon - light,
4. Beau - ti - ful Sav - ior! Lord of the na - tions!

O Thou of God and man the Son! Thee will I cher - ish,
Robed in the bloom - ing garb of spring: Je - sus is fair - er,
And all the twink - ling star - ry host: Je - sus shines bright - er,
Son of God and Son of Man! Glo - ry and hon - or,

Thee will I hon - or, Thou my soul's glo - ry, joy and crown!
Je - sus is pur - er, Who makes the woe - ful heart to sing.
Je - sus shines pur - er Than all the an - gels heav'n can boast.
Praise, ad - o - ra - tion Now and for - ev - er - more be Thine!

$\mathcal{L}$ittle is known of the origin of this cherished hymn. Associated with it are several popular legends which cannot always be substantiated by research. One of the best-known accounts is that it was called the "Crusaders' Hymn." Some think that it was sung by the twelfth century German Crusaders, especially by their children, as they made their long and wearisome trek to the Holy Land. Another account, which has more credence, is that it was one of the hymns used by the singing followers of John Hus, a small band of believers who settled in Silesia (now part of Poland) after they were driven out of Bohemia in the bloody anti-Reformation purge of 1620. This hymn, then, is generally said to be a folk song derived from these devout Silesian peasants.

The text for the hymn first appeared in the Roman Catholic *Munster Gesangbuch* of 1677, where it was published as the "first of three beautiful selected new hymns." Later it is said that a man by the name of Hoffman Fallersleben heard a group of Silesians singing the hymn in a service, recorded the words and music from this oral recitation, and published it in his *Schlesische Volkslieder* in 1842. This is the form in which we now know the hymn.

No one knows for certain who first translated the text from German into English. The English adaptation by Richard Storrs Willis, born in Boston, Massachusetts, on February 10, 1819, first appeared in his *Church Chorals and Choir Studies* in 1850. It is interesting to note that in this collection a notation about the origin of the hymn is made stating that it was "sung by the German knights on the way to Jerusalem." This statement undoubtedly did much to foster and popularize the Crusader account. Richard Willis is also the composer of the Christmas carol "It Came Upon a Midnight Clear."

The fourth verse, a fine translation by Joseph A. Seiss, emphasizes the dual nature of the Savior—"Son of God and Son of Man"—as well as the praise that will be eternally His.

"God has created man in His own image and therefore God is creative by His very nature. Because of this, man also has communication and expression as a basic part of his humanity. The characteristic common to God and man is the desire to make things as well as to enjoy the creation about him."

—Anonymous

6

God of Our Fathers

If my people, which are called by my name, shall humble themselves, and pray, and seek my face, and turn from their wicked ways; then will I hear from heaven, and will forgive their sin, and will heal their land.

—2 Chronicles 7:14

Author—Daniel C. Roberts, 1841–1907
Composer—George W. Warren, 1828–1902
Tune Name—"National Hymn"
Meter—10 10. 10 10

God of Our Fathers

Trumpets, before each stanza

1. God of our fa - thers, whose al - might - y
2. Thy love di - vine hath led us in the
3. From war's a - larms, from dead - ly pes - ti -
4. Re - fresh Thy peo - ple on their toil - some

hand   Leads forth in beau - ty all the star - ry
past.   In this free land by Thee our lot is
lence,   Be Thy strong arm our ev - er sure de -
way.   Lead us from night to nev - er - end - ing

band   Of shin - ing worlds in splen - dor thro' the
cast.   Be Thou our Rul - er, Guard - ian, Guide, and
fense.   Thy true re - li - gion in our hearts in -
day.   Fill all our lives with love and grace di -

skies,   Our grate - ful songs be - fore Thy throne a - rise.
Stay—   Thy Word our law, Thy paths our cho - sen way.
crease;   Thy boun - teous good - ness nour - ish us in peace.
vine;   And glo - ry, laud, and praise be ev - er Thine.

This stirring patriotic hymn has become increasingly popular since it was first written by an American Episcopalian minister, in 1876. Today it is included in nearly every published hymnal in this country. "God of Our Fathers" is the product of the Rev. Daniel C. Roberts, at that time pastor of a small rural church in Brandon, Vermont. It was written to commemorate the one hundredth anniversary of our country's Declaration of Independence and was sung for the first time at Brandon's Fourth of July celebration to the music of the old, Russian national anthem. This tune, which has since come to be known as the "Russian Hymn," is used exclusively today with the hymn "God the Omnipotent!" Later, Roberts submitted his text anonymously to the committee revising the Episcopal hymnal, and it was included in their 1892 edition, wedded with the "Russian Hymn" tune. At the time of our national Centennial observance commemorating the adoption of the Constitution, Robert's hymn text was chosen as the official hymn for that event. The committee commissioned the organist of the St. Thomas Episcopal Church in New York City, George William Warren, however, to compose an original tune for Robert's text. This new tune, with its dramatic trumpet calls before each stanza, contributed much to the growing popularity of the hymn. The hymn first appeared with its new tune, the "National Hymn," in 1894, in the official hymnal of the Episcopal Church, and Robert's text has been used exclusively with this music to the present time.

The hymn text represents Daniel Robert's one claim to literary fame. Evidently, he was a very modest man. In 1901, he wrote: "I remain a country parson, known only within my own small world." Concerning his hymn he once stated: "My little hymn has thus had a very flattering official recognition. But that which would really gladden my heart, popular recognition, it has not received."

Although popular recognition for Robert's hymn text was

slow in coming, he did receive various honors before his death in Concord, New Hampshire, on October 31, 1907. He was given a Doctor of Divinity degree by Norwich University, was made president of the New Hampshire Historical Society, as well as president of the State Normal School in Vermont, and Chaplain of the National Guard of New Hampshire. Following service in the Union Army during the Civil War and later ordination to the Episcopal ministry in 1866, Roberts served parishes in Vermont and Massachusetts, and for many years he was the vicar of the St. Paul's Church in Concord, New Hampshire.

The composer of the "National Hymn" tune, George William Warren, was known as an accomplished organist, while serving Episcopal churches in Albany, Brooklyn, and New York City. He also composed various anthems and hymn tunes and, in 1888, edited *Warren's Hymns and Tunes as Sung at St. Thomas' Church*. Later, Warren received an honorary Doctor of Music Degree from Racine College, in Wisconsin, in recognition of his church music accomplishments.

This text, with its recognition of God's providential guidance of our nation in the past and our need for reliance on Him for the future, combined with its stirring, inspirational music, is a very usable hymn for any national celebration.

7

Great Is Thy Faithfulness

*Every good gift and every perfect gift is from above,
and cometh down from the Father of Lights, with
whom is no variableness, neither shadow of turning.*

—James 1:17

Author—Thomas O. Chisholm, 1866–1960
Composer—William M. Runyan, 1870–1957
Meter—11 10. 11 10 with Chorus
Scripture Reference—Lamentations 3:22

Great Is Thy Faithfulness

*O*f the many gospel hymns written in recent times on the theme of God's goodness and faithfulness, this hymn stands out like a beacon light. While many hymns are born out of a particular dramatic experience, this hymn was simply the result of the author's "morning by morning realization of God's personal faithfulness."

Thomas Obadiah Chisholm was born in a humble log cabin in Franklin, Kentucky, on July 29, 1866. Without the benefit of high school or advanced training, he began his career as a school teacher at the age of sixteen in the same country schoolhouse where he had received his elementary training. When he was twenty-one, he became the associate editor of his hometown weekly newspaper, *The Franklin Favorite.* Six years later he accepted Christ as personal Savior during a revival meeting conducted in Franklin by Dr. H. C. Morrison. At Dr. Morrison's invitation Chisholm moved to Louisville to become office editor and business manager of Morrison's publication, the *Pentecostal Herald.* Later Chisholm was ordained to the Methodist ministry but was forced to resign after a brief pastorate because of poor health. After 1909 he became a life insurance agent in Winona Lake and later in Vineland, New Jersey. Thomas Chisholm retired in 1953 and spent his remaining years at the Methodist Home for the Aged, Ocean Grove, New Jersey.

Mr. Chisholm wrote more than 1200 poems, many of which have appeared frequently in such religious periodicals as the *Sunday School Times, Moody Monthly, Alliance Weekly,* and others. A number of these poems have become prominent hymn texts including the hymn "Living for Jesus."

In a letter dated 1941, Mr. Chisholm writes, "My income has not been large at any time due to impaired health in the earlier years which has followed me on until now. Although I must not fail to record here the unfailing faithfulness of a covenant-keeping God and that He has given me many wonderful displays of His providing care, for which I am filled with astonishing gratefulness."

In 1923 Mr. Chisholm sent several of his poems to the Rev. W. M. Runyan, a musician associated with the Moody Bible Institute and an editor with the Hope Publishing Company until his death July 29, 1957. Mr. Runyan has written as follows:

> This particular poem held such an appeal that I prayed most earnestly that my tune might carry over its message in a worthy way, and the subsequent history of its use indicates that God answered prayer. It was written in Baldwin, Kansas, in 1923, and was first published in my private song pamphlets.

This hymn was the favorite of the late Dr. Will Houghton, former beloved president of the Moody Bible Institute. It has since been an all-time favorite with students at the school, and as a result its usefulness has spread to evangelical churches everywhere. Bev Shea states that this hymn was first introduced to audiences in Great Britain in 1954 by the Billy Graham Crusades and has since been a favorite there as well.

He leads us on by paths we did not know;
Upward He leads us, though our steps be slow,
Though oft we faint and falter on the way,
Though storms and darkness oft obscure the day;
Yet when the clouds are gone,
We know He leads us on.
"He leads us on through all the unquiet years;
Past all our dreamland hopes, and doubts and fears,
He guides our steps, through all the tangled maze
Of losses, sorrows, and o'erclouded days;
We know His will is done;
And still He leads us on.
  —Nicolaus Ludwig, Count von Zinzendorf, 1700–1760

8

Have Thine Own Way, Lord!

But now, O Lord, Thou art our Father; we are the clay, and Thou our potter; and we all are the work of Thy hand.

—Isaiah 64:8

Author—Adelaide A. Pollard, 1862–1934
Composer—George C. Stebbins, 1846–1945
Tune Name—"Adelaide"
Meter—5.4.5.4 Doubled
Scripture Reference—Jeremiah 18:3–4

Have Thine Own Way, Lord!

1. Have Thine own way, Lord! Have Thine own way! Thou art the
2. Have Thine own way, Lord! Have Thine own way! Search me and
3. Have Thine own way, Lord! Have Thine own way! Wound-ed and
4. Have Thine own way, Lord! Have Thine own way! Hold o'er my

Pot - ter; I am the clay. Mold me and make me af - ter Thy
try me, Mas-ter, to - day. Whit-er than snow, Lord, wash me just
wea - ry, help me, I pray. Pow-er– all pow-er– sure-ly is
be - ing ab - so-lute sway! Fill with Thy Spir - it till all shall

will, While I am wait - ing, yield-ed and still.
now, As in Thy pres - ence hum-bly I bow.
Thine! Touch me and heal me, Sav - ior di - vine!
see Christ on - ly, al - ways liv-ing in me!

It really doesn't matter what you do with us, Lord—just have your way with our lives.

 *T*his simple expression, prayed by an elderly woman at a prayer meeting one night, was the source of inspiration that prompted the writing of this popular consecration hymn in 1902. From that time to the present, it has been an influential hymn in aiding individuals to examine and submit their lives to the Lordship of Christ.

The author of this hymn text, Adelaide A. Pollard, was herself experiencing a "distress of soul" during this time. It appears that it was a period in her life when she had been unsuccessful in raising funds to make a desired trip to Africa for missionary service. In this state of discouragement, she attended a little prayer meeting one night and was greatly impressed with the prayer of an elderly woman, who omitted the usual requests for blessings and things, and simply petitioned God for an understanding of His will in life. Upon returning home that evening, Miss Pollard meditated further on the story of the potter, found in Jeremiah 18:3–4:

Then I went down to the potter's house, and, behold, he wrought a work on the wheels. And the vessel that he made of clay was marred in the hand of the potter: so he made it again another vessel, as seemed good to the potter to make it.

Before retiring that evening, Adelaide Pollard completed the writing of all four stanzas of this hymn as it is sung today.

Adelaide Addison Pollard was known as a remarkable, saintly woman but one who lived the life of a mystic. She was born on November 27, 1862, at Bloomfield, Iowa. She was named Sarah by her parents, but because of her later dislike for this name, she adopted the name Adelaide. After an early training in elocution and physical culture, she moved to Chicago, Illinois, during the 1880s and taught in several girls' schools. During this time, she became rather well-known as an itinerant Bible teacher. Later, she became involved in the evangelistic ministry of Alexander Dowie, assisting him in his healing services. She, herself, claimed to have been healed of diabetes in this manner. Still later, she became involved in the ministry of another evangelist named Sanford, who was emphasizing the imminent return of Christ. Miss Pollard desired to travel and minister in Africa, but when these plans failed to materialize, she spent several years teaching at the Missionary Training School at Nyack-on-the-Hudson. She finally got to Africa for a short time, just prior to World War I, and then spent most of the war years in Scotland. Following the war, she returned to America and continued to minister throughout New England, even though by now she was very frail and in poor health. Miss Pollard wrote a number of other hymn texts throughout her life, although no one knows exactly how many, since she never wanted any recognition for her accomplishments. Most of her writings were signed simply AAP. "Have Thine Own Way, Lord!" is her only hymn still in use today.

The music for this text was supplied by George Coles Stebbins, one of the leading gospel musicians of this century. The hymn first appeared in 1907 in Stebbins' collection, *Northfield Hymnal with Alexander's Supplement.* That same year, it also appeared in two other popular hymnals, Ira Sankey's *Hallowed Hymns New and Old* and Sankey and Clement's *Best Endeavor Hymns.*

In 1876, George Stebbins was invited by D. L. Moody to join him in his evangelistic endeavors. For the next twenty-five years, Stebbins was associated with Moody and Sankey and such other leading evangelists as George F. Pentecost and Major D. W. Whittle as a noted song leader, choir director, composer, and compiler of many gospel song collections. George C. Stebbins lived to the age of ninety-one, passing away on October 6, 1945.

9

Holy, Holy, Holy

O come, let us worship and bow down: Let us kneel before the Lord our maker. For He is our God; and we are the people of His pasture.

—Psalm 95:6–7

Author—Reginald Heber, 1783–1826
Composer—John B. Dykes, 1823–1876
Tune Name—"Nicaea"
Meter—11 12, 12 10
Scripture Reference—Revelation 4:8–11

Holy, Holy, Holy

1. Ho - ly, ho - ly, ho - ly! Lord God Al - might - y!
2. Ho - ly, ho - ly, ho - ly! all the saints a - dore Thee,
3. Ho - ly, ho - ly, ho - ly! tho' the dark - ness hide Thee,
4. Ho - ly, ho - ly, ho - ly! Lord God Al - might - y!

Ear - ly in the morn - ing our song shall rise to Thee.
Cast - ing down their gold - en crowns a - round the glass - y sea;
Tho' the eye of sin - ful man Thy glo - ry may not see;
All Thy works shall praise Thy name in earth, and sky, and sea.

Ho - ly, ho - ly, ho - ly! mer - ci - ful and might - y!
Cher - u - bim and ser - a - phim fall - ing down be - fore Thee,
On - ly Thou art ho - ly— there is none be - side Thee
Ho - ly, ho - ly, ho - ly! mer - ci - ful and might - y!

God in three Per - sons, bless - ed Trin - i - ty!
Which wert, and art, and ev - er - more shalt be.
Per - fect in pow'r, in love, in pu - ri - ty.
God in three Per - sons, bless - ed Trin - i - ty!

Reginald Heber was born in the area of Cheshire, England, on April 21, 1783, of scholarly and well-to-do parents. At the age of seventeen he entered Oxford University, where his scholarship and literary abilities received much attention. Following his ordination to the ministry of the Anglican Church, he served for the next sixteen years at an obscure parish church in the little village of Hodnet in western England. Throughout his ministry he was known and respected as a man of rare refinement and noble Christian character. Heber was also noted as a prolific literary writer, making frequent contributions to magazines with his poetry, essays, and hymns.

In 1823, just three years before his early death at the age of forty-three, Heber was sent to India to serve as the Bishop of Calcutta. This responsibility included not only India but the Island of Ceylon and all of Australia as well. The pressures of this work along with the humid climate of that area wore heavily upon his health. One Sunday morning, after preaching to a large outdoor crowd of Indians on the subject of the evils of their caste system, he evidently suffered a sunstroke and died very suddenly. One year after his untimely death, a collection of his fifty-seven choice hymns was published by his widow and many friends. Most of these hymns are still in use today.

This hymn was written by Reginald Heber specifically for its liturgical use on Trinity Sunday, which occurs eight weeks after Easter. The emphasis of this Sunday's service is to reaffirm the doctrine of the triune Godhead. Though the word "trinity" is not found in the Scriptures, yet the truth of three Persons, equal and eternal with each other, is clearly taught throughout God's Word.

Reginald Heber is also the author of the hymn, "From Greenland's Icy Mountains."

The tune for this text has been named "Nicaea." It was named after the Council of Nicaea held in Asia Minor in A.D. 325, when the doctrine of the Trinity was examined and held to be a true and essential doctrine of the Christian faith. In 1861 this tune was composed specifically for these words by one of England's leading church musicians of the nineteenth century, Dr. John Bacchus Dykes. This popular composer has contributed more than 300 hymn tunes; most of them are still in use today.

Other hymns by John B. Dykes include "I Heard the Voice of Jesus Say," "Jesus, the Very Thought of Thee," "Eternal Father, Strong to Save," and "O for a Closer Walk With God."

10

How Great Thou Art

Great is the Lord, and greatly to be praised; and His greatness is unsearchable.

—Psalm 145:3

English Lyrics—Stuart K. Hine 1899–1989
Arrangement—Stuart K. Hine and Manna Music
Meter—11 10. 11 10 with Refrain

How Great Thou Art

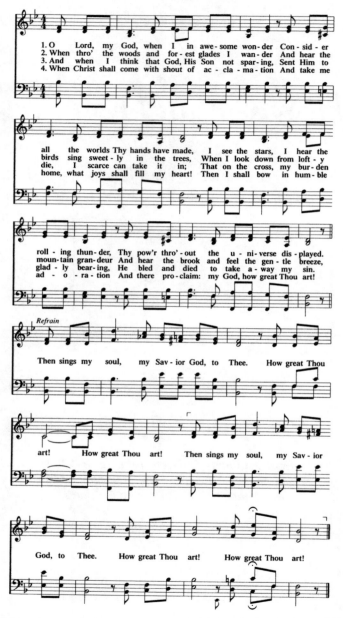

1. O Lord, my God, when I in awe-some won-der Con-sid-er
2. When thro' the woods and for-est glades I wan-der And hear the
3. And when I think that God, His Son not spar-ing, Sent Him to
4. When Christ shall come with shout of ac-cla-ma-tion And take me

all the worlds Thy hands have made, I see the stars, I hear the
birds sing sweet-ly in the trees, When I look down from loft-y
die, I scarce can take it in; That on the cross, my bur-den
home, what joys shall fill my heart! Then I shall bow in hum-ble

roll-ing thun-der, Thy pow'r thro'-out the u-ni-verse dis-played.
moun-tain gran-deur And hear the brook and feel the gen-tle breeze,
glad-ly bear-ing, He bled and died to take a-way my sin.
ad-o-ra-tion And there pro-claim: my God, how great Thou art!

Refrain

Then sings my soul, my Sav-ior God, to Thee. How great Thou

art! How great Thou art! Then sings my soul, my Sav-ior

God, to Thee. How great Thou art! How great Thou art!

This is a fine twentieth century hymn of praise that has become a favorite with God's people during the last three decades. Its popularity is due in large part to its wide use by favorite gospel singers, notably George Beverly Shea. Although introduced to American audiences when Mr. James Caldwell sang "How Great Thou Art" at Stony Brook Bible Conference on Long Island in 1951, it was not until Cliff Barrows and Bev Shea of the Billy Graham Evangelistic Team used it during the famed London Crusade in Harringay Arena that "How Great Thou Art" started to become universally well-known.

The original Swedish text was a poem entitled "O Store Gud," written by a Swedish pastor, the Reverend Carl Boberg, in 1886. In addition to being one of the leading evangelical preachers of his day, Boberg was also the successful editor of the periodical *Sanningsvittnet*. His inspiration for this text is said to have come from a visit to a beautiful country estate on the southeast coast of Sweden. He was suddenly caught in a midday thunderstorm with awe-inspiring moments of flashing violence, followed by a clear brilliant sun. Soon afterward he heard the calm, sweet songs of the birds in nearby trees. The experience prompted the pastor to fall to his knees in humble adoration of his mighty God. He penned his exaltation in a nine-stanza poem beginning with the Swedish words "O Store Gud, nar jag den varld beskader."

Several years later Boberg was attending a meeting in the Province of Varmländ and was surprised to hear the congregation sing his poem to the tune of an old Swedish melody.

The subsequent history of this hymn is most interesting. It is thought that soon after Boberg's version, the text was translated into German by Manfred von Glehn and entitled "Wie gross bist Du." Later in 1925 the Reverend E. Gustav Johnson of North Park College, Chicago, Illinois, made the first literal English translation from the Swedish text. This translation is quite different from the text that we know today but may still be found in some hymnals. Johnson's literal translation of the

Swedish text is entitled "O Mighty God. When I Behold the Wonder." In 1927 I. S. Prokhanoff came upon the German version and translated it into the Russian language.

In 1933 the Reverend S. K. Hine and his wife, English missionaries, were ministering to the people of the Ukraine. It was there they learned the Russian translation of "O Store Gud" from a congregation of Ukrainians. They remember singing it as a duet in dark, unevangelized places and the telling effect it had on the unsaved. The thought of writing original English lyrics to this song did not then occur to them—that was to await their crossing into Sub-Carpathian Russia, where the mountain scenery was to play its part. The thoughts of the first three verses in English were born, line upon line, amid unforgettable experiences in the Carpathian mountains. (The fourth verse was written later in England.) Thus, inspired partially by the Russian words, partially by the awesome wonder at the sight of "all the works thy hand hath made," the thoughts of the first two verses sprang into life in English. As Reverend Hine and his wife continued their evangelizing in the Carpathian mountains and distribution of gospels in village after village, verse three came into being.

When war broke out in 1939, it was necessary for Reverend Hine and his wife to return to Britain; now armed with these three verses, the writer continued his gospel campaigns during the "Blitz years." The fourth verse did not come until after the war.

The tune for this hymn is an arrangement made of an old Swedish folk melody. It is typically characteristic of many other hymn tunes, i.e., "Day by Day" with its lilting, warm, singable simplicity. With his original English lyrics and his arrangement of the Swedish folk melody, Mr. Stuart K. Hine published what we know today as the hymn "How Great Thou Art." Assignments of copyrights and publication rights to an American publishing firm in 1954 helped spread the popularity of this hymn. In April of 1974, *Christian Herald* magazine, in a poll presented to its readers, named "How Great Thou Art" the No. 1 hymn in America.

11

I Love to Tell the Story

The fruit of the righteous is a tree of life; and he that winneth souls is wise.

—Proverbs 11:30

Author—A. Katherine Hankey, 1834–1911
Composer—William G. Fischer, 1835–1912
Meter—13 7 6. 13 7 6. with Refrain

I Love to Tell the Story

1. I love to tell the story Of un-seen things a-bove,
Of Je-sus and His glo-ry, Of Je-sus and His love.
I love to tell the sto-ry Be-cause I know 'tis true.
It sat-is-fies my long-ings As noth-ing else can do.

2. I love to tell the story; More won-der-ful it seems
Than all the gold-en fan-cies Of all our gold-en dreams.
I love to tell the sto-ry, It did so much for me,
And that is just the rea-son I tell it now to thee.

3. I love to tell the story; 'Tis pleas-ant to re-peat
What seems each time I tell it More won-der-ful-ly sweet.
I love to tell the sto-ry, For some have nev-er heard
The mes-sage of sal-va-tion From God's own ho-ly Word.

4. I love to tell the story, For those who know it best
Seem hun-ger-ing and thirst-ing To hear it like the rest.
And when in scenes of glo-ry I sing the new, new song,
'Twill be the old, old sto-ry That I have loved so long.

Refrain

I love to tell the sto-ry! 'Twill be my theme in glo-ry
To tell the old, old sto-ry Of Je-sus and His love.

The evangelical emphasis or movement really began in England during the mid-eighteenth century with the ministries of such leaders as George Whitefield and John and Charles Wesley. The movement in its earliest days reached mainly the lower and middle classes of society with the upper classes remaining quite aloof from its influence. During the nineteenth century, however, the evangelical movement began to have considerable influence upon the upper classes as well. One such influential group was known as the Clapham Sect because the activities of this group centered in the elite suburb of Clapham in Southwest London. These men were wealthy evangelical philanthropists, students of the Bible, and men of prayer. They gave freely of their time, talents, and money to spread the gospel. Though these individuals generally maintained their membership within the Anglican Church, their emphasis was always on the necessity of personal conversion and guidance by the Holy Spirit rather than on a mere reliance upon the sacraments and rituals of the Church. There are numerous examples of the zealous ministries carried on by these influential Christian laymen, including a number of members of Parliament, who exercised great compassion upon the masses of impoverished people throughout the United Kingdom.

Katherine Hankey was born in 1834, the daughter of a wealthy English banker. Though the members of her family were prominent members of the Anglican Church, they were always associated with its more evangelical faction. Her father was one of the influential members of the Clapham Sect. Early in life Katherine, or Kate, as she was affectionately known, caught this same evangelical concern from her father. She began organizing Sunday school classes for rich and poor throughout London. These classes had a profound influence throughout the city with a large number of the young students in turn becoming zealous Christian workers. Kate also did considerable writing, including such works as *Bible Class Teachings*, a booklet on confirmation, as well as a number of books of verse. All of the royalties received from these publications were always directed to some foreign missions project.

When Katherine was only thirty years of age, she experienced a serious illness. During a long period of recovery she wrote a lengthy poem on the life of Christ. The poem consisted of two main sections, each containing fifty verses. The first section of the poem was entitled "The Story Wanted." It was from this part of her poem that she later adapted the words for another of her familiar hymn texts, "Tell Me the Old, Old Story." This hymn has since become another of the church's classic children's hymns.

Later that same year while still recovering from her illness, Kate Hankey completed the second part of her poem on the life of Christ. This sequel to the first section was entitled, "The Story Told." From these verses came the text for "I Love to Tell the Story," written in the same meter but with a different accent than her other familiar hymn text.

Being musically inclined, Kate also composed her own tunes for these two texts. Her hymns received little notice, however, when used with this music. The following year, 1867, a large international YMCA convention was held in Montreal, Canada. Major General Russell from England closed his emotionally charged message to the delegates by quoting Miss Hankey's two hymn texts. In the audience that day was William H. Doane, composer of more than 2,000 gospel songs. Mr. Doane was greatly moved by these lines and promptly composed musical settings for both texts.

Later a new musical setting, which replaced Doane's music for "I Love to Tell the Story," was composed by William G. Fischer, a Philadelphia piano dealer. Fischer also added the refrain for the hymn, "I love to tell the story! 'Twill be my theme in glory—to tell the old, old story of Jesus and His love." In 1875 the hymn appeared in Bliss and Sankey's collection, *Gospel Hymns and Sacred Songs,* which brought "I Love to Tell the Story" to the attention of congregations everywhere.

12

It Is Well with My Soul

God is our refuge and strength, a very present help in trouble.

—Psalm 46:1

Author—Horatio G. Spafford, 1828–1888
Music—Philip P. Bliss, 1838–1876
Meter—11 8 11 9 with Chorus

It Is Well with My Soul

1. When peace, like a riv - er, at - tend - eth my way, When sor - rows like
2. Tho Sa - tan should buf - fet, tho tri - als should come, Let this blest as -
3. My sin— O the bliss of this glo - ri - ous tho't— My sin, not in
4. And, Lord, haste the day when my faith shall be sight, The clouds be rolled

sea - bil - lows roll— What - ev - er my lot, Thou hast taught me to say,
sur - ance con - trol, That Christ hath re - gard - ed my help - less es - tate,
part, but the whole, Is nailed to the cross, and I bear it no more:
back as a scroll: The trump shall re - sound and the Lord shall de - scend,

CHORUS

It is well, it is well with my soul. It is well
And hath shed His own blood for my soul.
Praise the Lord, praise the Lord, O my soul! It is well
"E - ven so"— it is well with my soul.

with my soul, It is well, it is well with my soul.
with my soul,

This beloved hymn was written by a Presbyterian layman from Chicago named Horatio G. Spafford who was born in North Troy, New York, on October 20, 1828. As a young man Spafford had established a successful legal practice in Chicago. Along with his financial success, he always maintained a keen interest in Christian activities. He enjoyed a close and active relationship with D. L. Moody and other evangelical leaders of that era. He was described by George Stebbins, a noted gospel musician, as a "man of unusual intelligence and refinement, deeply spiritual, and a devoted student of the Scriptures."

Some months prior to the Chicago Fire of 1871, Spafford had invested heavily in real estate on the shore of Lake Michigan, and his holdings were wiped out by this disaster. Desiring a rest for his wife and four daughters as well as wishing to assist Moody and Sankey in one of their campaigns in Great Britain, Spafford planned a European trip for his family in November of 1873. Due to unexpected last minute business developments, he had to remain in Chicago, but he sent his wife and four daughters on ahead as scheduled on the S.S. *Ville du Havre.* He expected to follow in a few days. On November 22 the ship was struck by the *Lochearn,* an English vessel, and sank in twelve minutes. Several days later the survivors were finally landed at Cardiff, Wales, and Mrs. Spafford cabled her husband, "Saved alone." Shortly afterward Spafford left by ship to join his bereaved wife. It is thought that on the sea near the area where his four daughters had drowned, Spafford penned this text whose words so significantly describe his own personal grief—"When sorrows like sea billows roll . . ." It is noteworthy, however, that Spafford's hymn does not dwell on the theme of life's sorrows and trials but focuses attention in the third stanza on the redemptive work of Christ and in the fourth stanza anticipates His glorious Second Coming. Humanly speaking, it is amazing that one could experience such personal tragedies and sorrows as Horatio Spafford did and still be able to say with such convincing clarity, "It is well with my soul."

In 1881 the Spafford's fulfilled a life-long interest in the Holy Land. They left Chicago with their two young daughters and a group of friends and settled in Jerusalem. There they established the American Colony which cared for the sick and destitute. Although Horatio died just eight years later at the age of sixty, this significant ministry continued. The story of this special family and their ministry is told in the book, *Our Jerusalem,* written by the Spafford's daughter, Bertha Spafford Vesper.

Philip P. Bliss was so impressed with the experience and expression of Spafford's text that he shortly wrote the music for it, first published in one of the Sankey-Bliss Hymnals, *Gospel Hymns No. Two,* in 1876. Bliss was a prolific writer of gospel songs throughout his brief lifetime. In most cases he wrote both the words and music for his hymns. His songs, like most early gospel hymnody, are strong in emotional appeal with tunes that are easily learned and sung.

Other hymns by Philip P. Bliss include "Hold the Fort," "I Gave My Life for Thee," "Jesus Loves Even Me," "Let the Lower Lights Be Burning," and "Once for All."

13

Jesus Loves Me

And He took them up in His arms, put His hands
upon them, and blessed them.

—Mark 10:16

Author—Anna B. Warner, 1820–1915
Composer—William B. Bradbury, 1816–1868
Meter—77.77 with Chorus

Jesus Loves Me

1. Je - sus loves me! This I know, for the Bi - ble tells me so;
2. Je - sus loves me! He who died, heav - en's gate to o - pen wide,
3. Je - sus loves me! He will stay close be - side me all the way;

1. lit - tle ones to him be - long; they are weak, but he is strong.
2. he will wash a - way my sin, let his lit - tle child come in.
3. then his lit - tle child will take up to heav'n for his dear sake.

Refrain

Yes! Je - sus loves me! Yes! Je - sus loves me!

Yes! Je - sus loves me! The Bi - ble tells me so.

*W*ithout doubt the hymn that has influenced children for Christ more than any other is this simply stated one, written in 1860 by Anna Bartlett Warner. Miss Warner wrote this text in collaboration with her sister Susan as a part of one of the best-selling novels of that day, a novel written by Susan entitled *Say and Seal*. Today few remember the plot of that novel, which stirred the hearts of many readers. But the simple poem spoken by one of the characters, Mr. Linden, as he comforts Johnny Fax, a dying child, still remains the favorite hymn of children around the world to this day.

Anna and Susan Warner were highly educated and deeply devoted Christian young women who lived all of their lives along the Hudson River in New York, in a lovely but secluded area apart from the busy world. Their home was near the U.S. Military Academy at West Point, and for a number of years these two sisters conducted Sunday school classes for the young cadets. Their home, Good Crag, was willed to the Academy and made into a national shrine. Both sisters were buried with military honors in recognition of their spiritual contributions to the lives of the young military officers.

After the death of their widower father, a well-known New York lawyer, the Warner sisters were left with a meager income and of necessity turned to serious literary writing. Susan became especially noted for several of her works, including a popular book, *The Wide, Wide World*, considered at that time to be the best seller after *Uncle Tom's Cabin*. Although not as well-known as Susan for her literary fame, Anna wrote a number of novels under the pseudonym "Amy Lothrop" and published two collections of verse, *Hymns of the Church Militant*, 1858, and *Wayfaring Hymns, Original and Translated*, 1869.

The popularity of "Jesus Loves Me" soon spread quickly beyond the boundaries of our own land. Numerous stories are told by missionaries of the universal appeal this hymn text has had with children in every culture. It is often one of the first hymns taught to new converts in foreign lands. The hymn has even been appropriated by other religious sects; missionaries have reported that they have heard groups in Buddhist Temples singing, "Yes, Buddha loves me, Yes, Buddha loves me. . . ."

Dr. William B. Bradbury, the composer of the music for the text, was one of the important contributors to the development of early gospel hymnody in this country. He was born in York, Maine, on October 6, 1816. As a young man he moved to Boston, Massachusetts, where he became associated with Lowell Mason, often called the father of American public school and church music. Bradbury served as choir director and organist in several large Baptist churches in the East, where he became especially noted for his work with children. Among the highlights of his career were his annual Musical Festivals, where more than one thousand children would gather, all dressed alike, and sing many of his own compositions. Soon Bradbury gave himself exclusively to the teaching, writing, and publishing of a great volume of music. From 1841 until his death in 1868, he was involved with the publishing of fifty-nine collections of sacred and secular music. Bradbury composed the music for "Jesus Loves Me" in 1861 especially for Anna Warner's text and personally added the chorus to the four stanzas. It appeared in its present form in 1862 in his hymnal publication, *The Golden Shower.*

Other hymns by William B. Bradbury include "He Leadeth Me," "Just As I Am," "Depth of Mercy," "Even Me," "Sweet Hour of Prayer," and "The Solid Rock."

14

Joyful, Joyful, We Adore Thee

But the fruit of the Spirit is love, joy. . . .

—Galatians 5:22

Author—Henry van Dyke, 1852–1933
Music—Ludwig van Beethoven, 1770–1827
Tune Name—"Hymn to Joy"
Meter—87.87 Doubled

Joyful, Joyful, We Adore Thee

1. Joy - ful, joy - ful, we a - dore Thee, God of glo - ry, Lord of love;
2. All Thy works with joy sur - round Thee; Earth and heav'n re - flect Thy rays.
3. Thou art giv - ing and for - giv - ing, Ev - er bless - ing, ev - er blest,
4. Mor - tals join the might - y cho - rus Which the morn - ing stars be - gan.

Hearts un - fold like flow'rs be - fore Thee, Open - ing to the sun a - bove.
Stars and an - gels sing a - round Thee, Cen - ter of un - bro - ken praise.
Well - spring of the joy of liv - ing, O - cean depth of hap - py rest!
Fa - ther - love is reign - ing o'er us; Broth - er - love binds man to man.

Melt the clouds of sin and sad - ness; Drive the dark of doubt a - way.
Field and for - est, vale and moun - tain, Flow - ery mead - ow, flash - ing sea,
Thou our Fa - ther, Christ our Broth - er— All who live in love are Thine.
Ev - er sing - ing, march we on - ward, Vic - tors in the midst of strife.

Giv - er of im - mor - tal glad - ness, Fill us with the light of day!
Chant - ing bird and flow - ing foun - tain, Call us to re - joice in Thee!
Teach us how to love each oth - er; Lift us to the joy di - vine!
Joy - ful mu - sic leads us sun - ward In the tri - umph song of life!

This hymn is generally considered by hymnologists to be one of the most joyous expressions of hymn lyrics in the English language. Its author, Henry van Dyke, was born at Germantown, Pennsylvania, on November 10, 1852. During his lifetime he was recognized as one of the ablest Presbyterian preachers and leading liturgy figures in this country. In addition to achieving fame as a preacher, he served as a professor of literature at Princeton University from 1900–1923, was the moderator of his denomination, became a Navy chaplain during World War I, and represented his country as an ambassador to Holland and Luxembourg under an appointment by President Wilson. He was a prolific writer of devotional material with many of his books being best sellers.

This is the best-known of van Dyke's hymns. He stated his purpose in writing it as follows:

> These verses are simple expressions of common Christian feelings and desires in this present time, hymns of today that may be sung together by people who know the thought of the age, and are not afraid that any truth of science will destroy their religion or that any revolution on earth will overthrow the kingdom of heaven. Therefore these are hymns of trust and hope.

"Joyful, Joyful, We Adore Thee" portrays a joyful interplay between God's created world and the manifestation of this same creative spirit in the life of a believer. Such interesting similes as "hearts unfold like flow'rs before Thee . . ." illustrate this interesting technique. The second verse reminds us that all of God's creation speaks of His glory and, in doing so, directs our worship to the Creator Himself. The fourth stanza concludes with an invitation for all of God's children to join the mighty chorus of joy begun at creation's dawn (Job 38:7) and, in so doing, to find the encouragement needed for any circumstance of life.

The text for this hymn was written while van Dyke was a guest preacher at Williams College, Williamstown, Massachusetts. It is said that one morning van Dyke handed the manuscript to the college president, saying, "Here is a hymn for you. Your mountains (the Berkshires) were my inspiration. It must be sung to the music of Beethoven's 'Hymn of Joy.' It was first included in van Dyke's *Book of Poems,* third edition, published in 1911.

The tune, "Hymn of Joy," comes out of the final movement of Beethoven's Ninth Symphony, composed from 1817–1823, and published in 1826. Although Beethoven never wrote a tune specifically for a hymn text, a number have been adapted from his many famous works. This is the most widely used of these adopted hymn tunes. It was first adapted for a hymnal by Edward Hodges, an English organist who served the Trinity Church in New York City.

The Ninth or "Choral" Symphony was Beethoven's last symphony and is generally considered to be his greatest. It took him six years to complete the writing of this work. It was his supreme desire to complete one great symphony that would combine both instruments and voices in one majestic expression of sound. He was inspired for this work by a poem written by his German poet friend, Friedrich Schiller, a work entitled "Ode to Joy." It has always been a mystery to musicians to comprehend how Beethoven could conceive this work, as well as all of his great music that was composed after he was thirty years old, since at that age he became stone deaf. The account is given that when the Ninth Symphony was initially heard in Vienna, Austria, in 1824, the soloists had to come down from the stage and turn Beethoven around so that he could recognize the thunderous applause he was being given.

It is well said that the Bible contains very little humor, but it does have much to say about the importance of genuine joy in the life of each believer.

15

Lead On, O King Eternal

I *have fought a good fight, I have finished my course, I have kept the faith: Henceforth there is laid up for me a crown of righteousness, which the Lord, the righteous judge, shall give me at that day: And not to me only, but unto all them also that love His appearing.*

—2 Timothy 4:7–8

Author—Ernest W. Shurtleff, 1862–1917
Composer—Henry Smart, 1813–1879
Tune Name—"Lancashire"
Meter—76. 76 Doubled

Lead On, O King Eternal

1. Lead on, O King e - ter - nal, the day of march has come;
2. Lead on, O King e - ter - nal, till sin's fierce war shall cease,
3. Lead on, O King e - ter - nal, we fol - low, not with fears,

1. hence - forth in fields of con - quest thy tents shall be our home.
2. and ho - li - ness shall whis - per the sweet a - men of peace.
3. for glad - ness breaks like morn - ing wher - e'er thy face ap - pears.

1. Through days of prep - a - ra - tion thy grace has made us strong,
2. For not with swords' loud clash - ing, nor roll of stir - ring drums,
3. Thy cross is lift - ed o'er us; we jour - ney in its light;

1. and now, O King e - ter - nal, we lift our bat - tle song.
2. but deeds of love and mer - cy, the heaven - ly king - dom comes.
3. the crown a - waits the con - quest; lead on, O God of might.

$\mathcal{T}$his hymn was written by a young graduating seminarian, Ernest W. Shurtleff, in 1887. Shurtleff was born in Boston, Massachusetts, on April 4, 1862. His classmates at Andover Theological Seminary, recognizing the poetic ability of their colleague, asked him to write a hymn which they might all sing together for their commencement service. Shurtleff responded with this excellent text. At the time of his graduation he had already published two volumes of verse and throughout his later ministry wrote a number of additional hymns. This is his one hymn text, however, that has endured the passing of time.

Following his graduation from seminary, Shurtleff served, with distinction, Congregational Churches in California, Massachusetts, and Minnesota. During this time he was awarded the Doctor of Divinity Degree from Ripon College, Wisconsin. In 1905 he and his family went to Europe, where he organized the American Church in Frankfort, Germany. Later, in Paris, Shurtleff carried on a ministry with students and did relief work among the poor and needy. It was said that his entire life was truly the epitome of the hymn text he had written many years earlier for his own graduation service.

Although the metaphors and imagery used in this text were intended for their original purpose, the graduation, we can apply these truths to our personal lives and ministries today:

Verse One—   "days of preparation"—the time needed to pre-
              pare for the graduation hour from Seminary.
              "fields of conquest"—the specific responsibilities:
              pastorates to be assumed by these prospective
              ministers. "Thy tents . . ." speaks of the fact that
              the Christian minister is not called to a perma-
              nent abode but must be willing to move and live
              wherever God places him.
Verse Two—   Here is a summary of the whole purpose of
              the Christian ministry—warfare against sin, but

	always accomplished with "deeds of love and mercy."
Verse Three—	This is the motivation for Christian service—the sense of God's abiding presence throughout this life and the promised reward that awaits the faithful servant when his earthly task is complete.

The well-suited martial music for this text was borrowed by Shurtleff from a tune written fifty-two years earlier by an English organist and composer, Henry Smart. Smart originally composed this tune for the text "From Greenland's Icy Mountains" to be used at a musical festival at Blackburn, England, on October 4, 1835, observing the three-hundredth anniversary of the Reformation in England. "Lancashire," the name of this tune, is the county location of Blackburn, where Smart was organist at the time of this composition.

Henry Smart became well-known throughout England as a nineteenth-century composer, conductor, and compiler of sacred music, even though he spent the last fifteen years of his life in total blindness. Despite this affliction he continued his work as organist at St. Pancras Church, London, until his death in 1879. Another of his favorite tunes is used for the familiar Christmas carol, "Angels from the Realms of Glory."

16

A Mighty Fortress Is Our God

The Lord is my rock, and my fortress, and my deliverer; my God, my strength, in whom I will trust; my buckler, and the horn of my salvation, and my high tower.

Psalm 18:2

Author—Martin Luther, 1483–1546
English Translation—Frederick H. Hedge, 1805–1890
Composer—Martin Luther, 1483–1546
Tune Name—"Ein' Feste Burg"
Meter—87.87.66.667
Scripture Reference—Psalm 46

A Mighty Fortress Is Our God

Martin Luther was born on November 10, 1483, in Eisleben, Saxony, Germany. He was educated at the University of Erfurt, later becoming an Augustinian monk, teaching philosophy and theology at the University of Wittenberg. On October 31, 1517, sometimes called the "4th of July of Protestantism," Martin Luther nailed his ninety-five theses to the door of the Cathedral of Wittenberg, Germany. These theses condemned various practices and teachings of the Roman church. After several years of stormy disputes with the Pope and other church leaders, Martin Luther was finally excommunicated from the fellowship of the Roman Catholic Church in 1520.

One of the important benefits of the Reformation Movement was the rediscovery of congregational singing. Luther had strong convictions about the use and power of sacred music. He expressed his convictions in this way, "If any man despises music, as all fanatics do, for him I have no liking; for music is a gift and grace of God, not an invention of men. Thus it drives out the devil and makes people cheerful. Then one forgets all wrath, impurity and other devices." Again, "The Devil, the originator of sorrowful anxieties and restless troubles, flees before the sound of music almost as much as before the Word of God." In another place, "I wish to compose sacred hymns so that the Word of God may dwell among the people also by means of songs." Finally, Luther wrote, "I would allow no man to preach or teach God's people without a proper knowledge of the use and power of sacred song."

The single most powerful hymn of the Protestant Reformation Movement was Luther's "A Mighty Fortress Is Our God," based on Psalm 46. This hymn became the battle cry of the people, a great source of strength and inspiration even for those who were martyred for their convictions. This hymn has been translated into practically every known language and is regarded as one of the noblest and most classic examples of Christian hymnody. It is said there are no less than sixty translations of this text in English alone. In England the version by Thomas Carlyle is in general use, while in this country the translation by Frederick H. Hedge, a professor at Harvard University, is used most frequently. This translation was not made until 1852 and first appeared in a book entitled *Gems of German Verse* by W. H. Furness, published in 1853.

The first line of this national hymn of Protestant Germany is fittingly inscribed on the tomb of the great reformer at Wittenberg, and may still be read with appreciation by travellers to that historic spot.

17

O for a Thousand Tongues

Let every thing that hath breath praise the Lord.
Praise ye the Lord.

Psalm 150:6

Author—Charles Wesley, 1707–1788
Composer—Carl G. Glaser, 1784–1829
Tune Name—"Azmon"
Meter—CM (86.86)

O for a Thousand Tongues

1. O for a thou - sand tongues to sing My great Re - deem - er's praise, The glo - ries of my God and King, The tri - umphs of His grace!
2. Je - sus! the name that charms our fears, That bids our sor - rows cease; 'Tis mu - sic in the sin - ner's ears; 'Tis life, and health, and peace.
3. He breaks the pow'r of can - celled sin; He sets the pris - 'ner free. His blood can make the foul - est clean; His blood a - vailed for me.
4. He speaks, and lis - t'ning to His voice, New life the dead re - ceive. The mourn - ful, bro - ken hearts re - joice; The hum - ble poor be - lieve.
5. Hear Him, ye deaf; His praise, ye dumb, Your loos - ened tongues em - ploy. Ye blind, be - hold your Sav - ior come; And leap, ye lame, for joy.
6. In Christ, your Head, ye then shall know Shall feel your sins for - giv'n, An - tic - i - pate your heav'n be - low, And own that love is heav'n.
7. My gra - cious Mas - ter and my God, As - sist me to pro - claim, To spread thro' all the earth a - broad The hon - ors of Thy name.

It is generally agreed that Isaac Watts and Charles Wesley have been the two most influential writers of English hymnody to date. Following the new metrical psalmody introduced by Watts, the eighteenth-century Christian church was ready for the more warm, experiential hymns of Charles Wesley. God providentially raised Charles Wesley up to take the harp of Watts when the older poet laid it down and thus kept the church's song vibrant.

John and Charles Wesley, while students at Oxford University, formed a religious "Holy Club" because of their dissatisfaction with the spiritual lethargy at the school. As a result of their methodical habits of living and studying, they were jokingly called "methodists" by their fellow students. Upon graduation these young brothers were sent to America by the Anglican Church to help stabilize the religious climate of the Georgia Colonies and to evangelize the Indians.

On board ship as they crossed the Atlantic, the Wesley brothers came into contact with a group of German Moravians, a small evangelical group long characterized by missionary concern and enthusiastic hymn singing. The spiritual depth of these believers soon became evident during a raging storm. The following account is taken from Wesley's journal, January 25, 1736:

> In the midst of the Psalm wherewith their service began, the sea broke over, split the main sail in pieces, covered the ship and poured in between the decks. . . .
> A terrible screaming began among the English. The Moravians looked up, and without intermission calmly sang on. I asked one of them afterwards, "Were you not afraid?" He answered, "Thank God, no!"

John Wesley was so impressed with these people that he eventually made a detailed study of the hymnal used in their home church in Herrnhut, Germany. Soon he introduced a number of English translations of these Moravian hymns into the Anglican services. Between 1737 and 1786 the Wesleys published between them sixty-three hymnals, with many hymns of Moravian background.

Following a short and unsuccessful ministry in America, the disillusioned Wesleys returned to England, where once again they came under the influence of a group of devout Moravian believers meeting in Aldersgate, London. In May, 1738, both of these brothers had a spiritual heart-warming experience, realizing that though they had been zealous in the Church's ministry, neither had ever personally accepted Christ as Savior nor had known the joy of their religious faith as did their Moravian friends. From that time the Wesleys' ministry took on a new dimension and power.

Both John and Charles were endued with an indefatigable spirit, usually working fifteen to eighteen hours each day. Charles alone wrote no less than 6,500 hymn texts, with hardly a day or an experience passing without its crystallization into verse.

"O for a Thousand Tongues" was written in 1749 on the occasion of Charles's eleventh anniversary of his own Aldersgate conversion experience. It is thought to have been inspired by a chance remark by Peter Bohler, an influential Moravian leader, who exclaimed, "Had I a thousand tongues, I would praise Christ Jesus with all of them." The hymn originally had nineteen stanzas and when published was entitled, "For the Anniversary Day of One's Conversion." Most of the verses, no longer used, dealt in a very personal way with Wesley's own conversion experience.

Charles Wesley died on March 29, 1788, having spent more than fifty years in the service of the Lord he loved so intimately and served so effectively. Even as he lay on his death bed, it is said that he dictated a final hymn of praise to his wife.

Other hymns by Charles Wesley include "Christ the Lord Is Risen Today," "Jesus, Lover of My Soul," "A Charge to Keep I Have," "Depth of Mercy," and "Hark! The Herald Angels Sing."

18

The Old Rugged Cross

Who His own self bare our sins in His own body on
the tree, that we, being dead to sins, should live unto
righteousness: By whose stripes ye were healed.

—1 Peter 2:24

Author—George Bennard, 1873–1958
Composer—George Bennard, 1873–1958
Meter—Irregular with Chorus

The Old Rugged Cross

1. On a hill far a-way stood an old rug-ged cross, The em-blem of suf-f'ring and shame; And I love that old cross where the dear-est and best For a world of lost sin-ners was slain.

2. O that old rug-ged cross, so de-spised by the world, Has a won-drous at-trac-tion for me; For the dear Lamb of God left His glo-ry a-bove To bear it to dark Cal-va-ry.

3. In the old rug-ged cross, stained with blood so di-vine, A won-drous beau-ty I see; For 'twas on that old cross Je-sus suf-fered and died To par-don and sanc-ti-fy me.

4. To the old rug-ged cross I will ev-er be true, Its shame and re-proach glad-ly bear; Then He'll call me some day to my home far a-way, Where His glo-ry for-ev-er I'll share.

CHORUS

So I'll cher-ish the old rug-ged cross, the old rug-ged cross, Till my tro-phies at last I lay down; I will cling to the old rug-ged cross, the old rug-ged cross, And ex-change it some day for a crown.

Seldom can a song leader suggest a time for favorites from any congregation without receiving at least one request for "The Old Rugged Cross." This gospel hymn, a sentimental favorite of Christians and unsaved alike, was written by George Bennard in 1913. It is generally conceded to be the most popular of all twentieth century hymns.

George Bennard was born in Youngstown, Ohio, but his parents soon moved to Albia, Iowa, and later to the town of Lucas in the same state. It was here that young George made his personal acceptance of Christ as his Savior. Following the death of his father before George was sixteen years of age, he entered the ranks of the Salvation Army. Bennard and his first wife served for a period of time as officers in this organization.

Consequently, Bennard was ordained by the Methodist Episcopal Church, where his devoted ministry was highly esteemed. For some time he was busily involved in conducting revival services, especially throughout the states of Michigan and New York. One time, after returning to Michigan, he passed through a trying experience which caused him to reflect seriously about the significance of the cross and what the apostle Paul meant when he spoke of entering into the fellowship of Christ's suffering. As Bennard contemplated these truths, he became convinced that the cross was more than just a religious symbol but rather the very heart of the gospel. George Bennard has left the following account regarding the writing of this hymn:

> The inspiration came to me one day in 1913, when I was staying in Albion, Michigan. I began to write "The Old Rugged Cross." I composed the melody first. The words that I first wrote were imperfect. The words of the finished hymn were put into my heart in answer to my own need. Shortly thereafter it was introduced at special meetings in Pokagon, Michigan on June 7, 1913. The first occasion where it was heard outside of the

church at Pokagon was at the Chicago Evangelistic Institute. There it was introduced before a large convention and soon it became extremely popular throughout the country.

Shortly after writing this hymn, George Bennard sent a manuscript copy to Charles Gabriel, one of the leading gospel hymn composers of that era. Gabriel's prophecy, "You will certainly hear from this song," was soon realized as "The Old Rugged Cross" became one of the most widely published songs, either sacred or secular, in this country.

Bennard continued his evangelistic ministries for forty additional years following the writing of this hymn. He wrote other favorite gospel hymns, but none ever achieved the response of "The Old Rugged Cross." On October 9, 1958, at the age of eighty-five, Bennard exchanged his "cross for a crown." He spent the last years of his life by the "side of the road," a few miles north of Reed City, Michigan. Near this home there still stands a twelve foot high cross with the words, "'The Old Rugged Cross'—Home of George Bennard, composer of this beloved hymn."

Although it has often been stated that we do not worship the cross as such but rather the Christ of the cross, one cannot ponder the truths of Christ's atonement without a keen awareness of the centrality of the cross in God's plan of redemption for lost mankind.

19

Onward, Christian Soldiers

Thou therefore endure hardness, as a good soldier of Jesus Christ.

2 Timothy 2:3

Author—Sabine Baring-Gould, 1834–1924
Composer—Arthur S. Sullivan, 1842–1900
Tune Name—"St. Gertrude"
Meter—65.65 Doubled with Refrain

Onward, Christian Soldiers

1. On - ward, Chris - tian sol - diers! March - ing as to war,
2. At the sign of tri - umph Sa - tan's host doth flee;
3. Like a might - y ar - my Moves the Church of God.
4. Crowns and thrones may per - ish, King - doms rise and wane;
5. On - ward, then, ye peo - ple! Join our hap - py throng;

With the cross of Je - sus Go - ing on be - fore.
On, then, Chris - tian sol - diers, On to vic - to - ry!
Chris - tians, we are tread - ing Where the saints have trod.
But the Church of Je - sus Con - stant will re - main.
Blend with ours your voic - es In the tri - umph song.

Christ, the roy - al Mas - ter, Leads a - gainst the foe;
Hell's foun - da - tions quiv - er At the shout of praise;
We are not di - vid - ed; All one bod - y we:
Gates of hell can nev - er 'Gainst that Church pre - vail;
Glo - ry, laud, and hon - or Un - to Christ, the King:

For - ward in - to bat - tle, See, His ban - ners go!
Chris - tians, lift your voic - es, Loud your an - thems raise!
One in hope and doc - trine, One in char - i - ty.
We have Christ's own prom - ise, Which can nev - er fail.
This thro' count - less a - ges Men and an - gels sing.

Refrain

On - ward, Chris - tian sol - diers! March - ing as to war,

With the cross of Je - sus Go - ing on be - fore.

Baring-Gould was one of the truly gifted preacher-literary men of the nineteenth century. In addition to being ordained to the Anglican ministry in 1864, he was a noted writer throughout his life. His publications include eighty-five books on such varied subjects as religion, travel, folk-lore, mythology, history, fiction, biography, sermons, and popular theology. All are notable works. It is said that the British Museum shows more titles by him than by any other writer of this time. Yet, amazingly enough, the work for which Sabine Baring-Gould is best noted and remembered today is a simple children's hymn written in 1865.

The author has left the following account regarding the writing of this hymn:

> It was written in a very simple fashion, without thought of publication. Whitmonday is a great day for school festivals in Yorkshire, and one Whitmonday it was arranged that our school should join forces with that of a neighboring village. I wanted the children to sing when marching from one village to the other, but couldn't think of anything quite suitable, so I sat up at night resolved to write something myself. "Onward, Christian Soldiers" was the result. It was written in great haste.

Commenting on this hymn some thirty years later, Baring-Gould remarked, "It was written in great haste, and I am afraid that some of the rhymes are faulty. I am certain that nothing has surprised me more than its popularity."

One of the interesting verses not found in most hymnals shows the author's confidence for the endurance of the Church, based on such Scriptural promises as Matthew 16:18; 28:18–20:

> Crowns and throne may perish, kingdoms rise and wane,
> But the Church of Jesus constant will remain;

Gates of hell can never 'gainst that Church prevail;
We have Christ's own promise, and that cannot fail.

Another omitted verse indicates something of the author's personal convictions:

What the saints established that I hold for true
What the saints believed that believe I too.
Long as earth endureth men that faith will hold—
Kingdoms, nations empires, in destruction rolled.

A great hymn text must always be wedded to a fine tune in order to have universal appeal. Baring-Gould's hymn was first sung to the slow movement of Haydn's Symphony in D, No. 15, but that union has long since been forgotten. The present tune, "St. Gertrude," written by Sir Arthur S. Sullivan, was composed six years after the writing of the text. Sullivan, born in Bolwell Terrace, Lambeth, England, on May 13, 1842, was a noted English organist and composer. This tune was written in the home of a Mrs. Gertrude Clay-Ker-Seymer in Dorsetshire, England, while Sullivan was a guest there. He dedicated the music to his hostess and the tune is known as "St. Gertrude" to this day. Sullivan is also the composer of the well-known secular classic, "The Lost Chord," as well as a number of operettas such as *H.M.S. Pinafore* and *The Mikado,* done in collaboration with W. S. Gilbert, the librettist. These popular works have gained international fame.

The present version of this hymn was first published in America in John R. Sweney's *Gems of Praise,* by the Methodist Episcopal Book Room in Philadelphia, 1873.

Sabine Baring-Gould is also the author as well as composer of another very lovely children's hymn, "Now the Day is Over."

Despite his unceasing labors as a writer and preacher, Sabine Baring-Gould lived to the ripe old age of ninety years. He died in 1924, but his hurriedly written "Onward, Christian Soldiers" is still marching on from the lips of young and old alike.

20

Rock of Ages

Moreover, brethren, I would not that ye should be ignorant, how that all our fathers . . . did all drink the same spiritual drink; for they drank of that spiritual Rock that followed them: And that Rock was Christ.

—1 Corinthians 10:1, 4

Author—Augustus M. Toplady, 1740–1778
Composer—Thomas Hastings, 1784–1872
Tune Name—"Toplady"
Meter—77.77.77

Rock of Ages

1. Rock of A - ges, cleft for me, Let me hide my - self in Thee.
2. Could my tears for - ev - er flow, Could my zeal no lan-guor know,
3. While I draw this fleet-ing breath, When my eyes shall close in death,

Let the wa - ter and the blood, From Thy wound - ed side which flowed,
These for sin could not a - tone; Thou must save, and Thou a - lone.
When I rise to worlds un-known, And be - hold Thee on Thy throne,

Be of sin the dou - ble cure, Save from wrath and make me pure.
In my hand no price I bring; Sim - ply to Thy cross I cling.
Rock of A - ges, cleft for me, Let me hide my - self in Thee.

This hymn has traditionally been ranked as one of the most popular hymns ever written. It is certainly one of the best-known in the English language. It has been described as a "hymn that meets the spiritual needs of all sorts and conditions of men from the derelict snatched from the gutter by the Salvation Army to Prime Minister Gladstone, at whose funeral it echoed through the dim spaces of Westminster Abbey."

Whereas most hymns have been written out of some deep personal need or experience, this hymn evidently was born in a spirit of passionate controversy. Augustus Toplady was converted to Christ as a young boy of sixteen years of age while visiting in Ireland. Of his conversion Toplady has written,

> Strange that I, who had so long sat under the means of grace in England, should be brought right with God in an obscure part of Ireland, midst a handful of people met together in a barn, and by the ministry of one who could hardly spell his own name. Surely it was the Lord's doing and is marvellous.

For a time Toplady was attracted to the ministry of John and Charles Wesley and the Methodists. As time went on, however, he became a strong follower of the "election" doctrines of John Calvin and was vehemently opposed to the Arminian views promoted by the Wesleys and their supporters. By means of public debates, pamphlets, and sermons, Toplady and the Wesleys carried on theological warfare.

In 1776 Toplady published this hymn text in *The Gospel Magazine* as a climax to an article attempting to prove his argument that even as England could never pay her national debt, so man through his own efforts could never satisfy the eternal justice of a holy God. He entitled the hymn "A Living and Dying Prayer for the Holiest Believer in the World."

Some of the expressions in Toplady's hymn text are quite

obviously satirical swipes at such Wesleyan teachings as the need for contrite and remorseful repentance and the Arminian concept of sanctification—the belief that it is possible for any believer to live without consciously sinning and thereby to find the promised "rest," the state of moral perfection as described in Hebrews 4:9. Note Toplady's rebuttal in the second stanza:

> Could my tears forever flow, could my zeal no languor know, these for sin could not atone—Thou must save, and Thou alone.

Dr. Louis J. Benson, a noted hymnologist, in *Studies of Familiar Hymns,* calls attention to the fact that Toplady actually plagiarized his text from a hymn Charles Wesley had written thirty years earlier in a collection, *Hymns on the Lord's Supper.*

Augustus Montague Toplady was born at Farnham, England, on November 4, 1740, the son of Major Richard Toplady, who died in the service while his son was in infancy. Later young Toplady was graduated from Trinity College in Dublin, Ireland, and was ordained in 1762 to the ministry of the Anglican Church. His various pastorates included the French Calvinist Chapel at Leicester Fields, London, where he was known as a powerful and zealous evangelical preacher. Because of his frail constitution he died of overwork and tuberculosis at the early age of thirty-eight. Though known as a controversial preacher in his crusade against Arminian theology, Toplady was highly respected as a deeply spiritual, evangelical leader. His final statements just before his death are noteworthy: "My heart beats every day stronger and stronger for glory. Sickness is no affliction, pain no cause, death itself no dissolution. . . . My prayers are now all converted into praise."

The tune for Toplady's text was composed in 1830 by a well-known American church musician, Thomas Hastings. Hastings was the first musician of sacred music to dedicate his life to the task of elevating and improving the music of the churches in this country. He once wrote, "The homage that we owe Almighty God calls for the noblest and most reverential tribute that music can render."

Thomas Hastings was born on October 15, 1784, at Washington, Connecticut. Though his formal musical training was meager, and as an albino he was afflicted with eye problems throughout his life, yet he wrote no less than fifty volumes of church music, including 1,000 hymn tunes and more than 600 original hymn texts as well as editing more than fifty music collections. In 1858 the University of the City of New York conferred the degree of Doctor of Music upon him in recognition of his accomplishments. Along with Lowell Mason, Thomas Hastings is generally credited with being the person most instrumental in shaping the development of church music in the United States.

Other hymns by Thomas Hastings include "From Every Stormy Wind That Blows," "Majestic Sweetness Sits Enthroned," and "Come, Ye Disconsolate."

It is encouraging to realize that, despite the original belligerent intent behind this text, believers of both Calvinistic and Arminian theological persuasion can sing this hymn with spiritual profit and blessing.

21

Silent Night! Holy Night!

For unto you is born this day in the city of David a Savior, which is Christ the Lord.

Luke 2:11

Author—Joseph Mohr, 1792–1848
English Translation—John F. Young, 1820–1885
Composer—Franz Grüber, 1787–1863
Tune Name—"Stille Nacht"
Meter—Irregular

Silent Night! Holy Night!

1. Si - lent night! ho - ly night! All is calm, all is bright
2. Si - lent night! ho - ly night! Shep-herds quake at the sight;
3. Si - lent night! ho - ly night! Won-drous star, lend thy light.
4. Si - lent night! ho - ly night! Son of God, love's pure light

Round yon vir - gin moth-er and Child. Ho - ly In - fant, so ten-der and mild,
Glo - ries stream from heav-en a - far. Heav'n-ly hosts sing, "Al - le - lu - ia!
With the an - gels let us sing Al - le - lu - ia to our King.
Ra - diant beams from Thy ho-ly face, With the dawn of re - deem - ing grace,

Sleep in heav - en - ly peace; Sleep in heav - en - ly peace.
Christ the Sav - ior is born! Christ the Sav - ior is born!"
Christ the Sav - ior is born; Christ the Sav - ior is born.
Je - sus, Lord, at Thy birth, Je - sus, Lord, at Thy birth.

Joseph Mohr was born in the lovely city of Salzburg, Austria, in 1792. As a boy he was an active chorister in the Cathedral of Salzburg. In 1815 Mohr was ordained to the priesthood of the Roman Catholic Church. Following his ordination, he served various parishes in the Salzburg area. It was while serving as an assistant priest in 1818, at the newly erected Church of St. Nicholas in Obernorf in the region of Tyrol, high in the beautiful Alps, that Mohr wrote the text for this favorite of all Christmas carols.

Father Mohr and Franz Grüber, the village schoolmaster and church organist, had often talked about the fact that the perfect Christmas hymn had never been written. With this goal in mind, and after he had received word that his own church organ would not function, Father Mohr decided that he must write his own Christmas hymn immediately in order to have music for the special Christmas Eve Mass and to avoid disappointing his faithful congregation. Upon completing the text, he took his words to Franz Grüber, who exclaimed when he saw them, "Friend Mohr, you have found it—the right song— God be praised!"

Soon Grüber completed his task of writing the right tune for the new text. His simple but beautiful music blended perfectly with the spirit of Father Mohr's words. The hymn was completed in time for the Christmas Eve Mass, and Father Mohr and Franz Grüber sang their hymn to the accompaniment of Grüber's guitar. The hymn made a deep impact upon the parishioners, even as it has on succeeding generations. The passing of time seems only to add to its appeal.

Neither Mohr nor Grüber intended that their hymn would be used outside of their little mountain village area. However, it is reported that within a few days after the Christmas Eve Mass, the organ repairman, Karl Maurachen of Zillerthal, a well-known organ builder of that area, came to the church and obtained a copy of the new hymn. Through his influence the carol spread throughout the entire Tyrol region, where it became popular as a Tyrolean folk song. Soon various performing groups such as the well-known Strasser Children's Quartet began using the hymn in concert throughout Austria and Germany. In 1838 it first appeared in a German hymnal, where it was titled a "hymn of unknown origin." It was first heard in the United States in 1839 when a family of Tyrolean singers, the Rainers, used the music during their concert tour. Soon it was translated into English as well as into other languages. At least eight different English translations are known today. The carol is presently sung in all of the major languages of the world and is a universal favorite wherever songs of the Christmas message are sung.

The translation by John F. Young is the version most widely used in this country. Young was born at Pittston, Kennebec County, Maryland, on October 30, 1820. He was ordained to the Episcopal Church and served a number of years as a bishop in the state of Florida. Throughout his church ministry he had a keen interest in sacred music. This translation of Mohr's German text first appeared in 1863 in Clark Hollister's *Service and Tune Book*. In addition to this translation of this text, Young is also known as the editor of two published hymnals, *Hymns and Music for the Young,* 1861, and *Great Hymns of the Church,* published posthumously by John Henry Hopkins, 1887.

22

Take My Life and Let It Be

Whether therefore ye eat, or drink, or whatsoever ye do, do all to the glory of God.

—1 Corinthians 10:31

Author—Frances R. Havergal, 1836–1879
Composer—H. A. Cesar Malan, 1787–1864
Tune Name—"Hendon"
Meter—77.77

Take My Life and Let It Be

1. Take my life and let it be Con-se-crat-ed,
2. Take my hands and let them move At the im-pulse
3. Take my voice and let me sing Al-ways, on-ly,
4. Take my sil-ver and my gold— Not a mite would
5. Take my will and make it Thine— It shall be no
6. Take my love— my Lord, I pour At Thy feet its

Lord, to Thee. Take my mo-ments and my days— Let them
of Thy love. Take my feet and let them be Swift and
for my King. Take my lips and let them be Filled with
I with-hold. Take my in-tel-lect and use Ev-'ry
long-er mine. Take my heart— it is Thine own; It shall
trea-sure store. Take my-self— and I will be Ev-er,

flow in cease-less praise; Let them flow in cease-less praise.
beau-ti-ful for Thee, Swift and beau-ti-ful for Thee.
mes-sag-es from Thee, Filled with mes-sag-es from Thee.
pow'r as Thou shalt choose, Ev-'ry pow'r as Thou shalt choose.
be Thy roy-al throne; It shall be Thy roy-al throne.
on-ly, all for Thee, Ev-er, on-ly, all for Thee.

Frances Ridley Havergal, born on December 14, 1836, at Astley, Worcestershire, England, is often referred to as "the consecration poet." It has been said that the beauty of a consecrated life has never been more perfectly revealed than in her daily living. Wherever she saw spiritual and physical needs, Frances Havergal was there with genuine concern.

At the age of four she began reading and memorizing the Bible. At the age of seven she was already writing her thoughts in verse. She was greatly encouraged by her father, William Havergal, an influential Anglican clergyman, who for many years was involved in improving and composing English hymnody. Throughout her brief life Miss Havergal was frail and delicate in health, yet she was an avid student, writer, and composer. She learned several modern languages as well as Greek and Hebrew.

In her childhood years Frances lived in morbid fear that she would not be counted among God's elect. However, during early adolescence she had a vital conversion experience and later wrote, "There and then I committed my soul to the Savior—and earth and heaven seemed bright from that moment." She was a natural musician with a voice so pleasing that she was sought after as a concert soloist. She was also known as a brilliant pianist of the classics. Despite these musical talents, coupled with a vibrant personality offering possibilities for much worldly acclaim, her life's mission was to sing and work for Jesus.

"Take My Life and Let It Be" was written by Miss Havergal in 1874. She has left the following account:

> I went for a little visit of five days. There were ten persons in the house; some were unconverted and long prayed for, some converted but not rejoicing Christians. He gave me the prayer, "Lord, give me all in this house." And He just did. Before I left the house, everyone had got a blessing. The last night of my visit I was too happy

to sleep and passed most of the night in renewal of my consecration, and these little couplets formed themselves and chimed in my heart one after another till they finished with "ever only, ALL FOR THEE!"

In August, 1878, Miss Havergal wrote to a friend, "The Lord has shown me another little step, and, of course, I have taken it with extreme delight. 'Take my silver and my gold' now means shipping off all my ornaments to the church Missionary House, including a jewel cabinet that is really fit for a countess, where all will be accepted and disposed of for me."

While Frances Havergal was writing her many fine hymns in England, Fanny Crosby was also enriching lives with her numerous favorites. Although these two women never met, each was an ardent admirer of the other.

At the age of forty-two, when told by her physician that her physical condition was serious and that she did not have long to live, Miss Havergal replied, "If I am really going, it is too good to be true." At the bottom of her bed she had her favorite text placed where she could readily see it: "The blood of Jesus Christ His Son cleanseth us from all sin."

Frances R. Havergal is also the author of the hymn, "I Gave My Life for Thee" and "I Am Trusting Thee, Lord Jesus."

Cesar Malan, composer of this tune in 1823, was an ordained pastor of the State Reformed Church in Switzerland. Later he was dismissed from this church for his strong preaching against its formalism and spiritual apathy, and he became a fervent leader in his country for the evangelical faith. He was also a noted evangelist who made preaching tours of France, Belgium, and Great Britain. Although he wrote more than 1,000 hymn texts and tunes, he is remembered chiefly for this particular tune, "Hendon," thought to be named after a high hill near St. Paul's Cathedral in London, England. The tune first appeared in an American hymnal published by Lowell Mason in 1841.

23

Trust and Obey

And Samuel said, Hath the Lord as great delight in burnt offerings and sacrifices, as in obeying the voice of the Lord? Behold, to obey is better than sacrifice, and to hearken than the fat of rams.

—1 Samuel 15:22

Author—John H. Sammis, 1836–1919
Composer—Daniel B. Towner, 1850–1919

Trust and Obey

1. When we walk with the Lord In the light of His Word, What a
2. Not a shad-ow can rise, Not a cloud in the skies, But His
3. Not a bur-den we bear, Not a sor-row we share, But our
4. But we nev-er can prove The de-lights of His love Un-til
5. Then in fel-low-ship sweet We will sit at His feet, Or we'll

glo-ry He sheds on our way! While we do His good will, He a-
smile quick-ly drives it a-way. Not a doubt nor a fear, Not a
toil He doth rich-ly re-pay; Not a grief nor a loss, Not a
all on the al-tar we lay; For the fa-vor He shows And the
walk by His side in the way. What He says we will do; Where He

Refrain

bides with us still, And with all who will trust and o-bey.
sigh nor a tear Can a-bide while we trust and o-bey.
frown nor a cross But is blest if we trust and o-bey. Trust and o-bey,
joy He be-stows Are for them who will trust and o-bey.
sends we will go; Nev-er fear, on-ly trust and o-bey.

For there's no oth-er way To be hap-py in Je-sus But to trust and o-bey.

This favorite gospel hymn has long been cited as a choice example of a balanced biblical view of a believer's faith in Christ and the resultant good works that should then be evident. We begin with implicit trust in His finished redemptive work and then spend our lives seeking to obey Him and to fulfill, His revealed will in our daily living. Evangelist D. L. Moody once gave this formula for successful Christian living: "The blood alone makes us safe, the Word alone makes us sure, but obedience alone makes us happy."

The inspiration for this hymn came in 1886, during an occasion when Daniel B. Towner was leading music for Mr. Moody in Brockton, Massachusetts. Towner, the composer, has left the following account:

> Mr. Moody was conducting a series of meetings in Brockton, Massachusetts, and I had the pleasure of singing for him there. One night a young man rose in a testimony meeting and said, "I am not quite sure—but I am going to trust, and I am going to obey." I just jotted that sentence down, and sent it with the little story to the Rev. J. H. Sammis, a Presbyterian minister. He wrote the hymn, and the tune was born.

Upon receiving Mr. Towner's request, Mr. Sammis first composed the familiar lines of the refrain: "Trust and obey—for there's no other way to be happy in Jesus, but to trust and obey."

These lines became the capsule thought for the verses, which he then developed in the present five stanzas, detailing more fully the various areas of life that a believer must commit to the Lord, in order to be truly happy. The text with this tune first appeared in the collection, *Hymns Old and New,* published by the Revell Company, in 1887. It has been a favorite with God's people to the present time and has been translated into many foreign languages.

The author, John H. Sammis, was born on July 6, 1846, in Brooklyn, New York. At the age of twenty-three, he moved to Logansport, Indiana, where he became a successful business-man and an active Christian layman. Later, he gave up his business interests to serve as a YMCA secretary. Soon he felt called of God to enter the full-time Christian ministry. He attended McCormick and Lane Theological Seminaries, graduating from the latter in 1881. Following his ordination to the Presbyterian denomination, Sammis pastored churches in Iowa, Indiana, Michigan, Minnesota, and Indiana. In 1901, John Sammis moved to California to become a faculty member of the Bible Institute of Los Angeles. Here he died on June 12, 1919, having completed a lifetime of fruitful Christian service.

The composer, Daniel Brink Towner, was one who exerted a strong influence upon evangelical church music, both with his own compositions as well as in the training of other church music leaders. In 1890, Dwight L. Moody founded the Moody Bible Institute in Chicago, Illinois, for the express purpose of training evangelists and song leaders to carry on the work he had begun. Three years later, Towner was personally chosen by Mr. Moody to become the first head of the Music Department at the school, a position he had until his death in 1919. Daniel B. Towner is credited with more than 2,000 published songs, including such gospel favorites as "At Calvary," "Grace Greater Than Our Sin," "Saved by the Blood," "Nor Silver Nor Gold," "My Anchor Holds," "Anywhere With Jesus," and "Only a Sinner." In addition to his own gospel compositions, Mr. Towner was also associated with the publication of fourteen collections and hymnals as well as various textbooks on music theory and practice. As a teacher, he trained such notable musicians as Charles M. Alexander, Harry Dixon Loes, Homer Hammontree, H. E. Tovey, George S. Schuler, and many others. Daniel B. Towner's death occurred on October 3, 1919, no doubt as he would have desired it—while leading the music in an evangelistic meeting in Longwood, Missouri.

24

What a Friend We Have in Jesus

A *man that hath friends must show himself friendly:*
And there is a friend that sticketh closer than a brother.

—Proverbs 18:24

Author—Joseph Scriven, 1819–1886
Composer—Charles C. Converse, 1832–1918
Tune Name—"Converse"
Meter—87.87 Doubled

What a Friend We Have in Jesus

1. What a Friend we have in Je - sus, All our sins and griefs to bear!
2. Have we tri - als and temp-ta - tions? Is there trou-ble an - y - where?
3. Are we weak and heav-y - la - den, Cum-bered with a load of care?

What a priv - i - lege to car - ry Ev - 'ry-thing to God in prayer!
We should nev - er be dis - cour-aged— Take it to the Lord in prayer.
Pre - cious Sav-ior, still our ref - uge— Take it to the Lord in prayer.

O what peace we oft - en for - feit, O what need-less pain we bear,
Can we find a friend so faith - ful Who will all our sor-rows share?
Do thy friends de-spise, for - sake thee? Take it to the Lord in prayer;

All be - cause we do not car - ry Ev - 'ry-thing to God in prayer!
Je - sus knows our ev - 'ry weak-ness— Take it to the Lord in prayer.
In His arms He'll take and shield thee— Thou wilt find a sol - ace there.

$\mathscr{S}$omeone has well penned this statement, "A Christian's practical theology is often his hymnology." Many of us could attest to this truth as we recall some deeply moving experience—perhaps the loss of a dear loved one—and a simple hymn which has been used by the Holy Spirit to minister to our spiritual need.

Such a hymn is "What a Friend We Have in Jesus." Though it is not considered to be an example of great literary writing, its simply stated truths have brought solace and comfort to countless numbers of God's people since it was first written in 1857. So relevant to the basic spiritual needs of people are these words that many missionaries state that it is one of the first hymns taught to new converts. The very simplicity of the text and music has been its appeal and strength.

Joseph Scriven was born in 1819 of prosperous parents in Dublin, Ireland. He was a graduate of Trinity College, Dublin. At the age of twenty-five he decided to leave his native country and migrate to Canada. His reasons for leaving his family and country seem to be two-fold: the religious influence of the Plymouth Brethren upon his life estranging him from his family and the accidental drowning of his fiancée the night before their scheduled wedding.

From that time Scriven developed a totally different pattern of life. He took the Sermon on the Mount literally. It is said that he gave freely of his limited possessions, even sharing the clothing from his own body, if necessary, and never once refused to help anyone who needed it. Ira Sankey tells in his writings of the man who, seeing Scriven in the streets of Port Hope, Ontario, with his sawbuck and saw, asked, "Who is that man? I want him to work for me." The answer was, "You cannot get that man; he saws wood only for poor widows and sick people who cannot pay." Because of this manner of life Scriven was respected but was considered to be eccentric by those who knew him.

"What a Friend We Have in Jesus" was never intended by

Scriven for publication. Upon learning of his mother's serious illness and unable to be with her in far-off Dublin, he wrote a letter of comfort enclosing the words of this text. Some time later when he himself was ill, a friend who came to call on him chanced to see the poem scribbled on scratch paper near the bed. The friend read it with keen interest and asked Scriven if he had written the words. Scriven, with typical modesty, replied, "The Lord and I did it between us." In 1869 a small collection of his poems was published. It was simply entitled *Hymns and Other Verses.*

After the death of Joseph Scriven, also by accidental drowning, the citizens of Port Hope, Ontario, erected a monument on the Port Hope-Peterborough Highway, which runs from Lake Ontario, with the text and these words inscribed:

Four miles north, in Pengally's Cemetery, lies the philanthropist and author of this great masterpiece, written at Port Hope, 1857.

The composer of the music, Charles C. Converse, was a well-educated, versatile, and successful Christian, whose talents ranged from law to professional music. Under the pen name of Karl Reden, he wrote numerous scholarly articles on many subjects. Though he was an excellent musician and composer with many of his works performed by the leading American orchestras and choirs of his day, his life is best remembered for this simple music so well suited to Scriven's text.

Ira D. Sankey discovered the hymn in 1875, just in time to include it in his well-known collection, *Sankey's Gospel Hymns Number One.* Later Sankey wrote, "The last hymn which went into the book became one of the first in favor."

25

When I Survey the Wondrous Cross

And He *bearing* His *cross went forth into a place called the place of a skull, which is called in the Hebrew, Golgotha.*

—John 19:17

Author—Isaac Watts, 1674–1748
Music—From a Gregorian Chant
Arranged—Lowell Mason, 1792–1872
Tune Name—"Hamburg"
Meter—LM (88.88)
Scripture Reference—Galatians 6:14

When I Survey the Wondrous Cross

1. When I sur - vey the won - drous cross On which the
2. For - bid it, Lord, that I should boast, Save in the
3. See, from His head, His hands, His feet, Sor - row and
4. Were the whole realm of na - ture mine, That were a

Prince of Glo - ry died, My rich - est gain I
death of Christ, my God. All the vain things that
love flow min - gled down. Did e'er such love and
pres - ent far too small. Love so a - maz - ing,

count but loss, And pour con - tempt on all my pride.
charm me most, I sac - ri - fice them to His blood.
sor - row meet, Or thorns com - pose so rich a crown?
so di - vine, De - mands my soul, my life, my all!

This hymn by Isaac Watts, labeled by the well-known theologian Matthew Arnold as the greatest hymn in the English language, was written in 1707 for use at a communion service conducted by Watts. It first appeared in print that same year in Watts's outstanding collection, *Hymns and Spiritual Songs*. Its original title was "Crucifixion to the World by the Cross of Christ."

Isaac Watts was born on July 17, 1674, in Southampton, England. The eldest of nine children, he was the son of an educated deacon in a dissenting Congregational church. At the time of Isaac's birth, his father was in prison for his nonconformist beliefs. Young Watts showed an unusual aptitude for study and learned Latin at the age of five, Greek at nine, French at eleven, and Hebrew at thirteen. He began to write verses of good quality when he was very young.

Watts is frequently referred to as the father of English hymnody. One of his early concerns was the deplorable state to which congregational singing had degenerated in most English-speaking churches. The singing consisted of slow, ponderous Psalms in which each line was first read by an appointed deacon and was followed by the droning of the congregation. The texts of these Psalm-hymns were often crude and inelegant. Typical doggeral of the time is this:

> Ye monsters of the bubbling deep,
> > your Master's praises spout;
> Up from the sands ye coddlings peep,
> > and wag your tails about.

Watts once wrote, "The singing of God's praise is the part of worship most closely related to heaven; but its performance among us is the worst on earth." One Sunday after returning from a typically poor service, Watts continued to rail against the congregational singing. His father exclaimed, "Why don't you give us something better, young man!" Before the evening service began, young Isaac had written his first hymn, which was received with great enthusiasm by the people.

For a period of two years Watts wrote a new hymn every Sunday. He went on to write new metrical versions of the Psalms with a desire to "Christianize the Psalms with the New Testament message and style." Several of his hymns that were based on these new Psalm settings are such favorites as "Jesus Shall Reign" and "O God, Our Help in Ages Past." Watts is also the author of a children's hymn, "I Sing the Mighty Power of God."

Isaac Watts is also the author of "Am I a Soldier of the Cross?" and "Joy to the World!"

Watts also wrote a number of hymns based solely on personal feelings known as hymns of human composure. Such hymns were very controversial during his lifetime. "When I Survey the Wondrous Cross" is an example of this type of hymn written by Watts. In all Isaac Watts composed more than 600 hymns.

The tune for this text is known as the "Hamburg" tune. It was the work of Lowell Mason, who was often called the father of American public school and church music. Mason stated that he arranged this tune in 1824 from an ancient Gregorian chant, the earliest church music known. These church chants were inherited by the early Christians from the Hebrew Temple and Synagogue services. They represent some of the loveliest melodies known. Pope Gregory, who lived during the latter part of the sixth century, was one of the first church leaders to be concerned about church music. He did much to improve and organize these chants, hence the term "Gregorian Chants." These chants still form the basis of Roman Catholic Church music today. The "Hamburg" tune first appeared in the *Boston's Handel and Haydn Society Collection of Church Music* in 1825. It is interesting to note that the entire melody encompasses only a five note range.

Other hymns composed by Lowell Mason include "From Greenland's Icy Mountains," "Nearer My God, to Thee," "A Charge to Keep I Have," "Joy to the World!" "My Faith Looks Up to Thee," and "O Day of Rest and Gladness."